Afro-Arab Relations

Afro-Arab Relations

in the new world order

E. C. Chibwe

St. Martin's Press New York

 For information, write:
St. Martin's Press, Inc., 175 Fifth Avenue, New York, N.Y. 10010
Printed in Great Britain
Library of Congress Catalog Card Number 77-90935
ISBN 0-312-01063-x
First published in the United States of America in 1978

CONTENTS

LIST OF TABLES

ACKNOWLEDGEMENTS

The idea of writing this book was conceived in Sharjah during the Afro-Arab Syposium of December 1976. The Symposium was jointly sponsored by the University of Khartoum, the Federal Government of the United Arab Emirates and the Government of Sharjah. The participants were African and Arab scholars and writers. They were not representatives of States, Governments, or institutions and the views they expressed were personal and did not necessary reflect the institutions they serve.

These scholars and writers met to exchange views on how to bring about economic, cultural, scientific, social and political co-operation between Arabs and Africans. Eminent scholars on Arab and African affairs from the United States and Europe were initially invited as observers, but were later allowed to participate in the discussions.

The Symposium was formally opened by the Ruler of Sharjah, Sultan Bin Mohamed Al-Qasimi. To my surprise I was asked to reply to the Ruler's statement on behalf of all participants. I was also requested to present a paper on "Economic Co-operation between Arab and African States". I accepted with humility the privilege and honour accorded to me by my colleagues. When the time came to present the paper I decided not to read it but to speak off the cuff. At the end of my contribution Yusuf F. Hasan, Professor of History and Dean of the Faculty of Arts at the University of Khartoum urged me to write a book to elucidate the ideas and theories I had propounded. I had the will to do it, but time was my major constraint.

However, the idea came to fruition in March 1977. During my official leave, Professor Yusuf F. Hasan invited me to give a few lectures to his post-graduate students. My theme was "Triangular Co-operation between Africa, the Arab World and Europe". By the time I had taken leave of Khartoum I had decided on the form of this book.

The study relies heavily on field research which I did between July 1974 and December 1976. Arab and African diplomatic sources both in London and Europe were used extensively, but most of the material was obtained in the course of interviews. I thank all my diplomatic colleagues who furnished me with information.

My association with President Kaunda has been an invaluable asset to me. I cannot recount the number of times he recast my technical reports to reflect what I had in mind. He has extraordinary patience in listening to untried economic theories advanced by young Zambian economists. Ever since I left college he has been my mentor and intellectual guardian. I owe him a great debt of gratitude. My sincere thanks are also due to President Anwar Sadat who was kind enough to send me a personal letter thanking me for my contribution to the Afro-Arab cause reflected in my earlier book entitled *Arab Dollars for Africa*. He urged me to pursue the subject further. This study attempts to respond to the challenge of Afro-Arab co-operation.

The Ruler of Sharjah, Sultan Mohamed Al-Qasimi requires special mention. Despite his numerous duties as Head of State of Sharjah he found time to read my manuscript and provided me with technical advice and wisdom. His foreword to this book bears testimony to this assertion, and were it not for his assistance the book would not have materialised. I am, therefore, greatly indebted to him.

I wish to thank the rulers and officials of the United Arab Emirates and my colleagues who participated in the Symposium at Sharjah for their assistance in making it possible for me to complete the research.

I am grateful to Professor Ali Mazrui of the University of Michigan; Professor Alfred T. Moleah of the Temple University, Philadelphia; Professor A. Makapela of Princeton University, New York; Professor Mohamed Beshir of the University of Khartoum; and Professor A. Abuzayd of the University of Juba. I am also grateful to the officials of the Arab League, and of BADEA, and the staff of Khartoum University Library for providing me with essential data and to Miss Beatrice Chisela who typed my manuscript under what can best be described as extremely trying circumstances. Without their invaluable assistance this book would not have materialised. And I owe a particular debt of gratitude to Professor Yusuf F. Hasan who suggested that I undertake the research project in the first place.

Although the advice of all these people has been indispensable, I take sole responsibility for any errors of fact or interpretation that may remain. I owe a great deal to my wife and children for their sympathy and invaluable assistance rendered to me throughout the period I was engaged in writing, for without their understanding the book would not have been finished.

E. C. Chibwe, September 1977.

LIST OF ABBREVIATIONS

ADB:	African Development Bank
ADF:	African Development Fund
AFESD:	Arab Fund for Economic and Social Development
BADEA:	Arab Bank for Economic Development in Africa (sometimes abbreviated as ABEDIA)
BTU:	British Thermal Unit
ECA:	United Nations Economic Commission for Africa
EDF:	European Development Fund
EEC:	European Economic Community
EIB:	European Investment Bank
FAATA:	Fund for Arab-African Technical Assistance
FAO:	Food and Agriculture Organization
IBRD:	International Bank for Reconstruction and Development (World Bank)
IFAD:	International Fund for Agricultural Development
OAU:	Organization of African Unity
OAPEC:	Organization of Arab Oil-Producing Countries
OECD:	Organization of Economic Co-operation and Development
OPEC:	Organization of Oil-Producing Countries
SAFA:	Special Arab Fund for Africa
UNCTAD:	UN Conference on Trade and Development
UNDP:	UN Development Programme
UNIDO:	UN Industrial Development Organization

FOREWORD

by H.H. SULTAN BIN MOHAMED AL-QASIMI, Ruler of Sharjah and Dependencies

On 26 February 1977 brother Ephraim Chipampe Chibwe paid a courtesy call on me at Government House. Our discussion centred on the Afro-Arab Symposium which both of us had attended in December 1976, in my Emirate, Sharjah. In the course of our discussion, brother Chibwe reminded me that during the symposium participants had asked him to write a book on Afro-Arab relations. It was to be a follow-up to his earlier book, *Arab Dollars for Africa.* A letter from Professor Yusuf Fadl Hasan of the University of Khartoum confirmed that the participants had wanted me to write a foreword in my capacity as the Honorary President of Afro-Arab Symposium. As a keen and firm believer in Afro-Arab solidarity I accepted the solemn duty requested of me.

Brother Chibwe is one of the pioneers in the literature of Afro-Arab relations, and he has made several challenging proposals which require serious consideration by the policy-makers both in Africa and in the Arab World. Some of his proposals can be accommodated in the short-run; others will take time to put into effect, because they require some re-adjustments in the economies of Africa and the Arab World. And as we shall see, there are certain Afro-Arab schemes which can only be achieved through triangular co-operation between Africans, Arabs and the rest of the Third World.

I find brother Chibwe's treatise on Afro-Arab co-operation extremely interesting. It is not a litany of sins committed by either the Arabs or the Africans. It is not a one-sided enunciation of grievances. It does not sing the praises of one side for what it is doing for the other. It is simply a candid discourse on what Arabs and Africans genuinely believe to be the most important and urgent problems warranting their most immediate and serious consideration in areas of mutual interest: i.e. trade development, culture, finance, social links and international politics. The proposals are fair and reasonable, neither proposing more than what anyone deserves to get, nor demanding from anyone more than he can afford to give.

Because of their proximity it is natural that Africans and Arabs should co-operate. It would be odd for Arabs and black Africans to have no relationship when two-thirds of the Arab peoples live inside the African continent. Afro-Arab co-operation is not new. The Afro-Arab group manifested its solidarity at Bandung in 1955, in Belgrade in 1961 and in Cairo in 1964. They were able to work together because they had a common purpose and a common resolve and common potentialities. More recently, at the United Nations African nations have gone into the same lobby time and again with the Arabs over the questions of Israel, Zimbabwe, Namibia and South African racial policy. As brother Chibwe has rightly observed, relationships between Africans and Arabs reached a new level when African countries broke off diplomatic relations with Israel after the Israeli-Arab War of October, 1973.

Africans and Arabs have a unique opportunity of creating a structure of co-operation which alone will ensure the growth of interdependence between Africa and the Arab World. The recently concluded Afro-Arab Summit bears testimony to this belief. I know one thing for sure; we Arabs on our part are committed to working together with our African brothers. None of us can be indifferent to this commitment. As we coalesce in partnership, alliances, associations and various social systems in response to common bilateral or regional problems, we must now come together in creating a machinery for the implementation of Afro-Arab co-operation. The motivation is there. The institutions exist. Resources can be harnessed and pooled. What remains is for the two communities to translate theory into practice by fulfilling the inescapable tasks inherent in the co-operation they have aspired to attain.

The need to establish Afro-Arab co-operation cannot be over-emphasized. The challenge before us today is urgent and clear. It is to create a démarche that will replace our present timidity with resolve, our half-actions with bold programmes. Needless to say, prolonged passivity or neglect will not produce the desired co-operation. I make these observations on behalf of a nation that is prepared to play an active part in devising viable and practical measures for improving relations between Africa and the Arab World, within a framework formed by the realities of the world as it is, but in the interest of achieving a new international economic order.

I share brother Chibwe's belief that an accelerated economic growth of the developing countries requires an expansion of their production capacity and an improvement of their export possibilities. Almost all African and Arab countries depend heavily on production and export commodities. An international commodity policy will therefore have to be an important element in any serious effort to strengthen the economies not only of Africa and the Arab World but also of other Third World countries. This is where triangular co-operation becomes imperative. Like most leaders of the Third World I subscribe to the concept of a comprehensive approach to commodity problems. The objectives of an international commodity policy should be to stabilize the export earnings of developing countries at remunerative prices, to reduce price fluctuations and to promote stable supplies to the consumer. A successful implementation of an international commodities policy would contribute to the preservation of purchasing power and the terms of trade of developing countries.

Prophets of doom have been disappointed with the results of the Cairo Afro-Arab Summit Meeting. Before the meeting took place they case some doubt on its likely success. They were convinced that the sectional interests of each group would militate against the overall interests of the combined group. To their chagrin the conference was devoid of any confrontation; on the contrary it was characterized by solidarity and a unity of purpose between the two groups.

Brother Chibwe's historical analysis of the energy situation since the post-World-War-II period is bound to interest anyone concerned with the subject of Middle East oil. It is true that prior to 1973 prices of oil were kept artificially low, without any regard to the competitive standing of oil with respect to other sources of energy and to market forces. All the profits accrued to international companies, and these international companies were reluctant to plough back into Arab countries some part of the income earned in those States. It is also true that, if the OPEC countries had not increased oil prices in 1973 and 1974, energy demand trends would have continued unchecked into the future, depleting our oil resources by 1980. The increases in the price of oil have had a salutary effect on the energy demand and supply plans of industrialized countries. They have learnt to eliminate wastage, and have introduced conservation methods which were considered unnecessary when oil was unduly cheap.

It is essential that Afro-Arab co-operation should be a dimension of international co-operation, because the interests of Arab and African countries are interwoven with those of other members of the international community. It is common knowledge that the present economic system has not worked to build a just international society. We all recognize the need for changes to alleviate the present inequities, and want to participate in endeavours towards that end. The Cairo Afro-Arab Summit concluded on an important note, that real progress is possible if governments realize that economic and social developments should not be determined by unchecked economic forces. Arabs and Africans should without delay, as a first step in economic co-operation, dismantle all trade barriers as urged in the Cairo Declaration.

More than a decade and a half ago, all countries of the international community joined in declaring the 1960s, and then the 1970s, Decades of Development. The object of this declaration was to establish a new order in which the developing countries would finally share in the earth's abundance. These declarations of intent have only succeeded in whetting the appetite of developing countries would finally share in the earth's abundance. These declarations of intent

More than a decade and a half ago, all countries of the international community joined in declaring the 1960s, and then the 1970s, Decades of Development. The object of this declaration was to establish a new order in which the developing countries would finally share in the earth's abundance. These declarations of intent have only succeeded in whetting the appetite of developing countries. As a result of the pronouncements, the aspirations of the peoples of Africa and other Third World countries have risen, rather than diminished. But regrettably, this has not been matched by a corresponding commitment from developed countries. They have even failed to fulfil their pledge of transferring a meage 0.7 per cent of their GNP to developing countries. I am happy to say that the Arab oil-exporting countries have responded favourably to the United Nations call and have exceeded this target.

In conclusion I emphasize that the building of a new international society will require new thinking in the developed countries. It goes without saying that developed countries will have to accept changes in the structure of the international economy that will run counter to their vested interests. The peoples of the world must pledge themselves to a just international economic order. The task before us is difficult, but not insurmountable.

PREFACE

Taking the March 1977 Cairo Conference as the point of departure, this book examines the trends towards increased Afro-Arab co-operation in the past few years, the success of recent negotiations and the need for a more detailed analysis of the needs of both areas. The oil-price rises of 1973 created great financial wealth in Arab oil-producing countries but left many African countries in a state of disarray. The common political will to resolve the disparities was expressed in an atmosphere of solidarity in Cairo. What is needed now is a concerted effort to turn political will into concrete economic measures.

There are many areas of common political concern where the will to co-operate has been expressed on both sides. The most prominent current issues are the liberation of southern Africa and the resolution of the Middle East conflict between the Arabs and Israel. Since the Organization of African Unity and the Arab League respectively have these topics at the top of their regular agenda we examine the background of their programmes, both in the political and in the economic spheres. We also point out some of the present shortcomings of both the Arab League and the OAU in the hope that stumbling-blocks in the way of their co-operation may be identified and removed with the passage of time.

We then move on to summarize the economies of the Arab oil-producers and the use they have made of their increased oil revenues. There is much still to be done to stabilize the economies of these countries, and there are great demands on their resources; but a few of them still have enormous surpluses which should in our view be in part recycled into investment in Africa and elsewhere in the Third World. Ultimately it is not *aid* that the African Governments should seek from their Arab brothers but rather increased *investment* and *trade*. In considering future prospects for energy production and consumption we suggest the removal of the present restrictions on the flow of resources, both between the Arab World and the West and between the Arab World and Africa.

The economic interdependence of the World as a whole is a theme which we have attempted to develop. We thus juxtapose the bright prospects of the Arab World with the more gloomy prospects of Africa, where the possible ways out of the present economic difficulties are very restricted, but where there are avenues of hope in which Afro-Arab co-operation can be highly beneficial. Both parties can profit, not only in terms of their local interests, but in the interests of a new economic stability throughout the world.

The financial institutions for Afro-Arab co-operation are examined in detail, and consideration is given to the real needs of the less-developed countries. Foreign investment is a sensitive issue, but from a new kind of investment can come a multitude of rewards for African economies, especially if there is more concentration on infrastructure than at present.

Part II of this book takes the theme of Afro-Arab co-operation in the New International Economic Order a stage further, and we conclude by considering the need for solidarity between Africans and Arabs in world forums.

All in all we hope that by bringing together a wide range of up-to-date factual information on vital areas of the world economy we shall further the process of enlightenment about issues that affect all of us.

PART I

AFRO-ARAB CO-OPERATION

CHAPTER ONE

SUCCESSES OF THE AFRO-ARAB SUMMIT

The first important Afro-Arab Summit Conference, supported by 60 African and Arab States, took place in Cairo from 7 to 9 March 1977. It was the biggest single gathering of exporters of oil and raw materials. The Arab and African leaders concluded their summit by making economic and political policy declarations that, if implemented, could make the Arabs and Africans a joint force to be reckoned with in international forums. (See Appendix)

The conference was characterized by frankness. Delegates abandoned, if only temporarily, the language of diplomacy and made a marked effort to express their views plainly and openly. The most controversial discussions centred around the increases in oil prices, liberation movements in Africa and the Arab World, and Arab financial aid to Africa.

At the end of the conference Heads of State and Governments, or their authorized representatives, signed four documents on economic and political co-operation. The political declaration gave full support to the Palestinian cause, and advocated black majority rule in Zimbabwe, independence for Namibia and the French territory of the Afars and Issas, and an end to apartheid in South Africa. A further declaration on Afro-Arab co-operation pledged joint action in finance, mining, trade, industry, agriculture, energy, transport, communications and telecommunications. Two other documents covered the mechanics of co-operation including the need for the establishment of preferential trade agreements.

In a nutshell the Cairo Declaration, as it is officially known, was aimed at consolidating co-operation between African and Arab countries. The success of the conference was beyond the expectations of observers and participants alike. Observers had anticipated confrontation, and participants expected deadlock on most issues. What actually happened was that there was a large measure of agreement on most of the major issues submitted. Closing the meeting, President Anwar Sadat of Egypt said: 'I announce to the people of the World the full success of the Afro-Arab Summit which achieved its aims in realizing the hopes of our peoples on the African continent and in the Arab World.' President Sadat concluded his statement by telling the delegates that Afro-Arab co-operation had taken a great step forward from solidarity to cohesion.

There was a general consensus among the delegates that disagreement between Africans and Arabs had been kept to a minimum and that the emphasis of the Conference had been on discovering areas where co-operation was possible. President Kaunda was expressing the collective opinion of the delegates when he said that the Afro-Arab Summit Conference had been denigrated by foes and cynics who had sought to highlight the divergence of views and regional interests, not the unity of purpose. But this had not prevented the African and Arab leaders from achieving unity and co-operation far beyond their own expectations. Similar sentiments were voiced by Presidents Barre of Somalia, Nimeiry of Sudan and Ahidjo of Cameroon.

Liberation movements in Africa and the Arab World were well represented, and during the conference liberation leaders were given the opportunity to discuss their problems with individual leaders of Arab and African States. Arafat, the leader of the Palestinian Liberation Organization, met President Kaunda, who pledged his support for the PLO. He said that the cause for which the Palestinian people were fighting was a just one and could not be ignored. In reply, Arafat thanked Dr Kaunda for the support Zambia was giving to his organization and assured him that the PLO would continue fighting until the battle was won.

A dominant theme of most of the speeches was that colonialism must be wiped out of Africa and the Arab world. There was general agreement too that the economic and political involvement of two of the super-powers in the Middle East and in southern Africa gravely complicated the situations there. Israel was accused of giving material aid and military expertise to the racist regime in South Africa, enabling them to bolster the special military operations of the illegal regime in Zimbabwe. All these considerations led to a general recognition of the fact that a co-ordinated Afro-Arab programme of action and commitment was called for.

The delegates condemned the vetoes that had been cast in the UN by Western countries on resolutions concerning South Africa, Rhodesia and Namibia. Such vetoes clearly indicated the importance the Western powers attach to the minority regimes in southern Africa, seeing them as essential to the preservation of the existing world economic order.

By far the most controversial question discussed at the conference was that of oil prices. This is something which has been raised at every single meeting between Africans and Arabs since 1973, when the oil-producing countries decided to increase their prices by more than 100 per cent. At that time the decision was met with great concern by the entire community of Third World non-oil-producing countries, who were alarmed by the prospect of extensive damage to their weak economies.

The response of OPEC has been to argue that the decision to raise the price of oil was not made with the intention of harming the economies of Third World countries. On the contrary, it was designed to pressurize the industrialized countries into paying reasonable prices for raw materials — many of which come from developing countries — and so could be seen as advantageous, in the long term, to the developing world. What they were not willing to do was to apply a system whereby they would charge lower prices for oil sold to developing countries. This was because the bulk of this oil was channelled through multinational corporations, which are controlled from Western industrialized nations; it was, they argued, the multinationals who would derive maximum benefit from a two-tier price system. The best way of alleviating the situation was to provide some kind of subsidy to the countries who were most seriously affected by the oil-price increase. In practice, this method of giving subsidies benefited Asia more than Africa.

By October 1976 however, news had leaked out that OPEC countries were going to increase the price of oil again, this time by as much as 30 per cent. The Western industrialized countries used it as an excuse to delay reaching decisions at the 'North-South Dialogue' which was then taking place in Paris.

They argued that until they knew how much they were going to spend on oil they were unable to decide on the official development assistance they would offer to developing countries. They asked non-oil-producing nations of the Third World to try to dissuade OPEC from further increasing the price of oil, arguing that any rise of more than 5 per cent would plunge the world economy into another recession and would have an adverse effect on their own already damaged economies. This was already only too clear to the countries of the developing world. Most of them had already abandoned ambitious development projects in order to pay for the earlier increase in the price of oil and other imported commodities.

It is important to observe here that it was not only the price of oil which rose sharply at this time but also that of other essential commodities. In Zambia for example almost all essential commodities imported into the country had gone up by an extraordinary percentage, partly as a result of increased transport costs which reflect world-wide inflation.

At the December 1976 OPEC meeting in Doha, however, the participating countries did not raise prices by as much as had been feared. Two nations, Saudi Arabia and the United Arab Emirates, who are the major Middle Eastern oil producers, resolved to apply a rise of only 5 per cent in 1977, while the eleven other OPEC members raised prices by 10 per cent.

Saudi Arabia's Oil Minister, Sheikh Ahmed Zaki Yamani, explained after the Doha meeting that he had called for a moderate price rise to avert renewed inflationary pressures that might trigger further economic recession in the West — which would have harmful consequences for the economic development and industrialization of the oil producers themselves, as they would suffer from price increases on imported goods. It was a decision praised by Zambia's President Kaunda, among others.

On the other hand several African countries were critical of the 10 per cent rise by the other eleven OPEC nations. The Tanzanian *Sunday News* said in an editorial that the burden of oil-price rises falls on the poor countries of the Third World: the rich West would only export the burden of higher oil prices via increased prices of machinery, medicines or consumer goods. Nevertheless the OPEC Special Fund for the less developed countries was immediately increased by an additional $700 million, to take it to a total of $1.5 billion, and more aid was promised in the following months, notably at the Cairo Afro-Arab Summit in March.

The Cairo Summit was an opportunity for these and other points to be raised and some of the differences to be resolved. Notably the Arabs pledged to contribute an extra $1.5 billion specifically to help economic development in Africa. At a press conference after the Summit, the Chairman of the recently established Arab Bank for Economic Development in Africa (BADEA), Chedly Ayari, said that his organization and the African Development Bank (ADB) would soon be meeting to discuss the distribution of the promised funds.

The Summit ended with an agreement to establish an ad hoc Commission to provide the framework for closer political and economic co-operation. The conference also approved political and economic declarations laying down the principles for such co-operation. The Commission will be formed from within the Arab League and the Organization of African Unity, and will be responsible for the creation of special working groups to study specific areas of co-operation such as trade, mining, energy and agriculture. It will also monitor progress on an 11-point, long-term plan for economic and financial co-operation that includes the encouragement of Arab investment in Africa. The conference also agreed that a Summit should be held once every three years, with a ministerial meeting of OAU and Arab League members every eighteen months.

One of the problems which may arise is that few African States are likely to have fully worked-out proposals ready to submit for possible funding. This being the case it may well be a long time before all the funds are allocated, and some may even remain at the time of the next Afro-Arab Summit. If this were to happen it would support the argument, put forward by some Arab leaders, that most African countries have not yet developed an infrastructure capable of accommodating new industries financed by Arab oil revenue. It is therefore up to African states to respond promptly to the challenge.

THE AFRO-ARAB SYMPOSIUM

A few months before the Cairo Summit, an Afro-Arab Symposium was held in Sharjah in the United Arab Emirates. The Secretary-Generals both of the Organization for African Unity and of the Arab League were represented and the participants discussed the draft Declaration and the Afro-Arab joint action programme which had been approved, in July 1975, by the Afro-Arab Ministerial Committee. The Declaration recommended that the OAU and the Arab League should be the bodies responsible for the implementation of joint Afro-Arab policies — as was agreed at Cairo. The symposium identified the following objectives to be pursued by the two organizations:

1. Elimination of the vestiges of colonialism still existing in the Arab world and in the southern part of the African continent. This means giving full support to African and Arab liberation movements.
2. Rejection of neo-colonialism in the Arab world and in the African continent, by adopting unified economic and political policies. This would entail close contacts between intellectuals and politicians of the African and Arab communities in order to make it possible for the two groups to arrive at common goals.
3. Eradication of backwardness, and economic liberation from the ex-colonial countries. The Afro-Arab Movement should undertake an international role in this respect through participating in the solution of world problems and carrying out effective measures for liberating the African economy, while adopting a joint strategy for altering the international balance of power.

The symposium emphasized the need for the relations between the Arab League and the OAU to be based on clear-cut principles with a definition of objectives and programmes. Empty and sometimes meaningless slogans would simply do injustice to the two organizations. Economic co-operation was identified as one of the major objectives of Afro-Arab relations. The symposium observed that care should be taken to ensure that economic co-operation should be carried out through a systematic, well-structured and renewable framework after acquiring full knowledge of the development needs of Africa, with a reciprocal African knowledge of the real requirements of the Arab countries.

Two areas were singled out as being of special importance: first, that the principles of co-operation should not be made to depend on African countries being obliged to repay Arab favours by supporting them on all issues; second, that Afro-Arab co-operation should be dynamic and able to adapt to a changing world. In order for this to be possible, information would need to be freely and widely available and in this regard the symposium proposed the establishment of information centres in Africa and the Arab World. His Highness Sheikh Sultan Bin Mohamed Al-Qasimi, member of the Supreme Council and Ruler of Sharjah, donated a luxurious new hall in Sharjah to be used as an Information Centre and a Conference Hall for Afro-Arab meetings. The hall has been named 'Africa Hall'.

Participants at the Sharjah Symposium thus concentrated on strengthening the foundations of Afro-Arab political unity. It was left to the Cairo Summit for concrete economic proposals to be made. Before going on to look in more detail at the economic conditions existing in the African and in the Arab world, and at the financial institutions which can play a role in economic co-operation between the two communities, it is important to examine more closely the political considerations which make this co-operation a realistic proposition.

CHAPTER TWO

STRENGTHENING POLITICAL CO-OPERATION

The Afro-Arab history of the twentieth century would be incomplete if it failed to record the unselfish work of Presidents Nasser and Nkrumah. These two, individually and collectively, were responsible for a new spirit of freedom, a re-awakening of self-assertion and of policies for self-reliance among Afro-Arab people. This Afro-Arab awareness produced Afro-Arab solidarity.

At the non-aligned conferences in Bandung in 1955, Belgrade in 1961 and Cairo in 1964, the main pre-occupation of the States present was to pursue a declared programme for peace and international co-operation and above all the elimination of colonialism in the countries of the Third World. The theme of decolonization was highlighted at the Cairo Conference in 1964. The conference felt the need for urgent collective action for the liberation of dependent countries. The countries present undertook to give all necessary support, moral, financial and military, to freedom fighters in territories under colonial rule — which included Zimbabwe, Angola, Mozambique, Namibia, Guinea Bissau and South Africa.

During the early 1960s Cairo was the venue and centre for Afro-Arab and Afro-Asian discussion on economic co-operation, international trade and economic aid for and among developing countries. One could say that the idea of the new international economic order originated in the Cairo Conference of 1964. It was natural for Afro-Arab re-awakening to take place in Cairo, the capital of Egypt. This was the land of the pyramids and the Pharaohs, the base of the Arab League and Arab nationalism. And Egypt had a national leader whose influence was felt and appreciated throughout Africa and the Arab World.

Gamal Abdel Nasser's dynamism and dedication were an inspiration, and his political objectives were loud and clear. He was concerned with the unity of the Arab World and the decolonization of the African continent. He recognized that to achieve these objectives he would need international moral support outside the Arab World and Africa; hence Egypt's active role in the non-aligned movement, where it emphasized the need for Third World solidarity. Nasser was among the first Arab leaders to recognize the need to help African liberation movements. He wrote that the Arab World could not stand apart while 5 million whites harass 200 million people in Africa '. . . for one important obvious reason — we ourselves are in Africa — we cannot under any conditions relinquish our responsibility to spread the light of knowledge and civilization up to the very depth of the virgin jungles of the continent.'

Kwame Nkrumah, the founder of modern Ghana and the conjurer of Pan-Africanism, was a contemporary of Nasser. The two leaders shared similar ideals of Pan-Africanism and African unity. Their efforts towards decolonization were not restricted to Africa and the Arab World. They also channelled their energies to other countries of the Third World that were struggling for survival and freedom from the economic, political and social fetters of imperialism. Their message is still valid today.

It is important to remember the early efforts at forging solidarity between the Arab World and Africa, because there is a mistaken but common view that the present co-operation between Arabs and Africans is based purely on expedience and self-interest. It has been suggested that the Arabs have held out offers of loans and financial aid to the African States purely to get diplomatic support against Israel — or, *mutatis mutandis*, that the African States broke off their diplomatic relations with Israel only in the hope of gaining rich financial rewards from the Arabs. Such a view of the Afro-Arab relationship is a distorted one and the proof will come when there are concrete results. Co-operation can only succeed when it is based on mutual trust and respect and not on material or monetary considerations. Present Afro-Arab co-operation can be said to be based on 'discrimination in favour of your brother'. The decision announced at the UN General Assembly on 4 October 1973 by President Mobutu Sese Seko, when he said that faced between the choice of supporting a friend (Israel) and a brother (the Arab World) he had no choice but to support the brother, expressed the African view adequately.

Certain basic trends and conceptions have influenced African countries individually and collectively to support the Arab cause. Some Arab countries are located in Africa and are members of the OAU, taking an active part in its work. The Charter of the OAU considers Africa as one geographical entity, and an attack on a member-State of the OAU is considered to be an attack on the Organization as a whole. The OAU has therefore had an obligation to give support to member-States involved in the Arab-Israel conflict. As early as June 1971 the OAU adopted a resolution calling for appropriate diplomatic measures against Israel. This resolution led to the establishment of a committee of ten Heads of State comprised of Cameroon, Ethiopia, Ivory Coast, Kenya, Liberia, Mauritania, Nigeria, Senegal, Tanzania and Zaire. A sub-committee of Senegal, Zaire, Cameroon and Nigeria was mandated to mediate between Israel and the Arabs. Although the initiatives of this sub-committee did not produce peace in the Middle East, its success lay in being the first outside organization to establish simultaneous contact with the Arab and Israeli adversaries.

A further illustration of solidarity was provided by the Kenyan Government in the years following the 1973 oil-price rises. Members of Parliament and journalists in Nairobi have regularly criticized the Arabs for making life difficult for those in the less-developed countries, despite the fact that Africa had shown solidarity with the Arab cause. But the Finance Minister, Mwai Kibaki, reminded Parliament that Kenya severed diplomatic relations with Israel not for financial gain but as a matter of principle. Among the intellectuals who shared his views was Professor Ali Mazrui, a former head of department of Political Science at Makerere University in Uganda. Professor Mazrui refused to subscribe to the theory that because Africans severed diplomatic ties with Israel after 1973 they were automatically entitled to direct Arab financial and economic aid. He argued that while Africa may have ostracized Israel in 1973 because she was the enemy of the Arabs, it was also the case that the Arabs had at no stage established any form of relationship with South Africa and

Rhodesia, who were the enemies of Africa. He further noted that Egypt and Algeria used to help Africa liberation movements long before the rights of Palestinians were recognized by most of the African States.

LIBERATION MOVEMENTS IN AFRICA

The liberation of southern Africa and certain parts of the Arab World from the yoke of colonialism is a specific objective of Arab-African co-operation. One can even go so far as to say that Arab-African solidarity is a vital necessity in the struggle against colonial and racist regimes.

In various international forums the nationalists of Zimbabwe, Namibia and South Africa and the Palestinians have all stated publicly that their struggles have both internal and external features with similar and common characteristics. The Arabs say that the Palestinian people are confronted with the problem of Zionism. They argue that the Zionist philosophy is based on a belief in the Jews' racial superiority as the 'chosen children of God' over the Palestinian people or over other races of the world, and that the Zionists have, by force, displaced the Palestinian people and exiled them from their native land. The African nationalists in southern Africa say that they suffer from a similar fate. The regimes in southern Africa have adopted the philosophy of apartheid. They regard the black race as inferior. Like the Palestinian Arab, the South African black has been deprived of the wealth of his country, and he has been forced to live in small crowded areas called 'Homelands' which are merely arid border lands, incapable of supporting them.

Both African and Arab nationalists refer to the unacceptable and unholy alliance between Zionism, apartheid and world imperialism. They contend that without the support of world imperialism both Zionism and apartheid would have neither base nor strength to support them. The imperialist world, in its own economic interests, provides Zionism and apartheid with weapons and huge sums of money to support their economies. The nationalists also contend that there is evidence of strong ties between Zionism in Israel and apartheid in southern Africa. And it is true that, for the past few years, the

General Assembly of the United Nations has expressed serious concern at the political, economic and military relations between the two countries.

The South African Prime Minister paid an official visit to Israel from 9 to 12 April 1976 which culminated in the conclusion of an agreement on co-operation in various fields between the two countries. The UN Ad-Hoc Committee on Apartheid was perturbed by this visit and subsequently decided to prepare a preliminary report on the growing co-operation between the two countries, to be sent to the General Assembly and the Security Council, and also to the OAU, the non-aligned Conference and the Arab League. On 11 August 1976, Ambassador Leslie A. Harriman of Nigeria, Chairman of the Ad-Hoc Committee on Apartheid, took advantage of the presence in Sri Lanka of the Heads of States of several non-aligned countries to denounce the reported sale by Israel of missile boats to South Africa.

Israel and South Africa derive considerable benefits from their alliance: they have much in common and their political survival can only be prolonged if they co-operate in creating differences both among African countries and between African and Arab countries. There are economic benefits which accrue to both parties: Israel by obtaining raw materials and South Africa by increasing its exports. Mutual cultural programmes have enhanced their ideological similarities. And in the military field, the alliance provides Israel and South Africa with additional sources of arms and technical knowledge, apart from confidential information on strategy and tactics. Press reports state that military co-operation between South Africa and Israel has been in existence for some time. It is supposed to go back as far as the time when the state of Israel was born, and it is alleged that South Africa played a big role in the 1973 war. The Egyptian Government declared that a South African Mirage was downed on the Suez Canal front during the war.

There is a story currently circulating to the effect that there is new co-operation between Israel and South Africa through military equipment supplies and training aids related to guerrilla war and the use of sophisticated weapons. Other reports indicate that Israel may provide South Africa with the Israeli-made Gabriel sea-missiles and missile boats. Senior Israeli military officers have also paid regular visits to South Africa to deliver lectures on modern fighting methods and guerrilla warfare. On 3 April 1976 the *Daily Telegraph* correspondent in Johannesburg reported that Israeli officers had assisted the South African Army during its military operation in Angola.

LIBERATION MOVEMENTS REQUIRE SUPPORT

To counteract the alliances of their enemies, liberation movements have had to develop their relationships with states and international organizations. It is extremely difficult to organize and fight a liberation war purely from within the country to be liberated. Nationalist movements in South Africa, Zimbabwe and Namibia for example, have used Zambia and Tanzania as bases for their military wings and political headquarters, although for the host countries there are risks. For her generosity, Zambia has paid heavily in terms of human lives and the disruption of her economy. The nationalist movements in southern Africa get some of their financial and material assistance from the OAU via its Liberation Committee based in Tanzania.

Recently the liberation movements have been urged to unite in order to consolidate their efforts and to conserve limited funds from the OAU member-states, who are supposed to contribute according to their ability to pay. In cases where liberation movements have failed to unite, the OAU has chosen to make contributions either to the dominant movement or to the one most active on the battlefield. The Heads of States of the 'frontline' countries (Tanzania, Mozambique, Angola, Botswana and Zambia) followed this principle when agreeing to support only the 'Patriotic Front' in Zimbabwe.

Apart from assistance from the OAU, African liberation movements have received most of their material support (for arms, clothing etc.) from sources outside Africa such as the USSR and the People's Republic of China, although this is usually in limited quantities.

The Palestinian movement for its part does not have financial problems because the Arab States who give it material and moral support are currently affluent in monetary terms. They also consider the Palestinian cause to be important for the whole Arab World, and feel it natural to support it to the full, even to the extent of providing it with additional army personnel. To all intents and purposes, the Palestinian movement is a military wing of the Arab World. Many Arab States make provision for contributions to the Palestinian movement in their national budgets. Both the Palestinian and the African liberation movements have gained diplomatic recognition through their contact with the UN General Assembly and Security Council. They have succeeded in legitimizing their own activities and have managed, with some success, to isolate the enemy.

There is an increasing alliance between the African and Arab liberation movements. On several occasions the African liberation movements have sent delegates to visit the fighting forces of the PLO, and in turn PLO delegates have visited offices of the African liberation movements. Liberation movements often speak on behalf of others. Moreover when one liberation movement comes across vital information concerning one of the enemies this information is conveyed to the movement concerned.

The unity of the nationalist movements has facilitated the work of the Arab League and the OAU in preparing common strategies. Thus African States severed diplomatic relations with Israel in 1973 and some African countries have been giving material and moral assistance to the PLO. Similarly some Arab countries have imposed an oil embargo on South Africa and a total embargo on Rhodesia and have supported UN resolutions on Namibia.

RESOLVING THE MIDDLE EAST CONFLICT

The consensus of experts on Middle East conflict is that after three decades of war and crises in that area, the time is now ripe to resolve the conflict. It is not only that some measure of political contact has been established between the adversaries but, more important, that chances for promoting a peaceful settlement between Israel and its Arab neighbours are better than before because the parallel conflict of the two superpowers has been temporarily submerged or suspended. This is partly because America and the Soviet Union want to make progress on the important question of strategic arms limitation, and partly because the Soviet Union's influence in the Middle East is at a low ebb.

James Abourezk, the first Arab-American Senator in US history, has observed a slight shift in American understanding of the Arab viewpoint since he came to Washington in 1970. He attributes the change to the 1973 oil embargo and the fact that Arab countries are an economic power that the United States cannot afford to ignore.

The hope for a settlement in the Middle East is shared by several Arab leaders like President Sadat of Egypt and King Khaled of Saudi Arabia. Since the United States now seems to enjoy the confidence of the main parties to the conflict, a rare opportunity has arisen for American diplomacy. If Washington can play its cards properly the Middle East conflict can be resolved to the benefit of all parties concerned, including the two major powers.

The United States has acquired an important ally in Saudi Arabia. Having abandoned the old strategy of acting through puppet governments, the United States now selects countries which are recognized in their own right as leaders in their respective regions, such as Brazil in South America, Japan in Asia, Nigeria in black Africa and Saudi Arabia in the Middle East. As far as Saudi Arabia is concerned, many Arabs are happy with the choice. Saudi Arabia is not dependent on US aid, and it is best suited at the moment to be the spokesman for the Arab States. It is the largest supplier of foreign oil to the United States; its decision in 1976 to hold down the price-increase of oil will help keep inflation down in America; and above all, the Saudis have announced that they will increase their production from 8.5 million to 11.8 million barrels of crude oil a day. While the United States will be the main consumer of this additional supply, it is felt that the United States should reciprocate the Saudi's gesture by influencing Israel to make meaningful concessions.

By 1977 the Arab States had agreed to recognize Israel's right to exist on condition that Israel withdrew from the Arab territories which she had occupied since the 1967 war: the Sinai peninsula which is Egyptian territory; the Gaza Strip, formerly administered by Cairo; the West Bank of the River Jordan and East Jerusalem, which were taken from the Kingdom of Jordan; and the Golan Heights, a part of Syria. The Arabs have further demanded that a new State, populated by Palestinian Arabs, be created on the West Bank and in Gaza.

Some influential Israelis have come to accept the fact that a withdrawal would be in their own interest; but the majority of Israelis still contend that Israel must keep key position in these territories, to safeguard herself from future attacks. This fear could be taken care of by a UN peace-keeping force which could be stationed along Israel's borders with a provision that it would only be withdrawn by unanimous vote of the Security Council. With that guarantee, the United States, the foster-parent, could veto any untimely withdrawal of the peace-keeping troops.

Because of the magnitude of the Middle East conflict it has become necessary for the United Nations to be involved in the search for solutions; but its efforts have not produced the desired results. It is well-known that the UN is effective as a peace-maker only when the parties concerned want peace themselves. The United Nations can only guide the different parties, it cannot impose any decision on them. Secretary General Kurt Waldheim admits that he has no illusions about the UN's ability to solve the Middle East conflict on its own. It requires the contributions and efforts of the Co-Chairmen of the Geneva Conference (the US and the USSR), and of course the full co-operation of the Arabs and the Israelis.

Recent voting at the UN has indicated that European countries are also keen to find a lasting peace in the Middle East. In 1976 the EEC countries voted with the US on only five resolutions, supporting two, opposing two and abstaining on one. Fayez Sayegh, Kuwait's Adviser on Palestinian Affairs at the UN, says that the European states showed a considerable change in their attitude towards the Arab cause in 1976, voting more often in favour of resolutions supporting the Arab case. He calculated that, whereas in 1975 13% of the votes cast were in favour, 33% were against and 53% were abstentions, in 1976 the figures were 38%, 18% and 48% respectively.

THE ARAB LEAGUE AND THE OAU

Both Arabs and Africans have long aspired to unity of their respective parts of the world, but the efforts made in this direction have not met with success. During and since the colonial era, unity has been one of the objectives of liberation movements. When a leader such as Nkrumah achieved independence for his country, he sought also to unite Africa. He believed that the independence of Africa or the Arab World was incomplete unless it was followed by complete unity of the member-states of the regions concerned. This ideal is still far from being realized, and it is clearly true that the time is not ripe for absolute unity. One does not need to be a student of African or Arab political history to be aware of several instances of recent conflict among member-States of both the Arab League and the OAU.

The term 'co-operation' is in tune with past and present realities much more than the term 'unity'. There has long been co-operation of various degrees and kinds between the Arabs and Africans. Several visits have been undertaken by leaders of either side during which co-operation agreements relating to political and commercial matters have been signed. Meanwhile there have been continuing efforts to bring about economic harmonization amongst countries sharing common borders within each of the regions under study. Some have met with serious setbacks, as for example the East African Community; but others have grown in significance through careful and practical preparation, such as the Economic Community of West African States, which although still in its infancy promises to bring about more equitable development in the countries of the region than has been the case up to now.

Because both the Arabs and the Africans are forging their co-operation with instruments which were designed to serve different purposes it has taken a long time for them to have a proper meeting of minds on issues of mutual interest. The time taken to bring about the Summit meeting between Arab and African Heads of State proves the point. It was in Mogadishu in 1973 that the idea of an Afro-Arab Summit meeting was conceived. It is inherent in man to resist change and to oppose ideas which have not been tried elsewhere. Change is often associated with unknown danger, failure or conflict. It was therefore not surprising that the original idea of a Summit meeting between Arab and African Heads of State was received with mixed feelings. Those present say that the going was hard and slow because the parties were wary, at times hostile. They say that there was fear of deceit or double-talk. As expected, each side had its own concept of co-operation. After several years of delay the Afro-Arab Summit finally took place in March 1977 only because of the increasing political will of both sides.

The new relationship between the two communities should be more lasting because it is more enlightened and more scientifically planned. And both the OAU and the Arab League can play an important part although in their present form the two bodies are not equipped to undertake the additional responsibilities.

At the time when these two organizations were formed, the idea of Afro-Arab co-operation was in embryo, so neither Charter has inscribed in it anything specific about Afro-Arab relations. The Arab League Charter was drawn up in 1945 by half a dozen independent States. The OAU Charter was drawn up in 1963 when there were 36 independent states. At the time of writing there are 20 members of the Arab League and 48 members of the OAU. Thus in both organizations there are many States which did not participate in the original founding procedures. Time has moved on and the aims and roles of these bodies are very different from when they were first conceived.

The two organizations are not often staffed by the best talents available. The Secretary-General in each institution is an administrative official. He is not free to pick his staff. In essence the two institutions make decisions relating to both policy and administrative matters, and the Secretary-General does what others feel is appropriate. If he wants to engage the services of Mr X from country Z because X has special professional qualifications and experience relevant for the job he may be told that the job should be given to P because his country is not represented on the Secretariat. Talent does not count as much as geography, and this can be a drawback. Moreover, each Charter was primarily designed to deal with purely Arab or purely African questions. But now the two organizations have come to accept the fact of international interdependence. Indeed this is a first principle of diplomatic activity today. Policies directed at a fruitful arrangement in this respect constitute a real hope for peace and stability in international relations, so the need to amend the two Charters has become imperative.

The Cairo Afro-Arab Summit agreed to set up an ad hoc Commission to provide the framework for closer economic and political co-operation between the Arab League and the OAU. This Commission will make recommendations to a Summit meeting of the OAU and the Arab League in respect of the changes to be undertaken either separately or jointly for the purpose of implementing co-operation in all areas between the two organizations. The leaders of the member-States of the two bodies should be assured that the distinctive features of the two organizations will not suffer, but would rather be enhanced. A good example to follow is the co-operation of ACP States. African, Caribbean and Pacific countries did not lose any of their individual characteristics when they formed the ACP Group in negotiation with the European Economic Community — and with their new collective bargaining power they secured far more beneficial agreements than could have been possible before.

We believe that under the present circumstances co-operation is an objective for immediate implementation, while unity should be a more distant ideal. We recognize that co-operation will not come about without difficulties; but we believe that such difficulties will not be insurmountable because they will be easily identifiable, whereas it is not possible to know what storms the proposals of unity will have to weather. We would like to think that co-operation will be a stepping-stone to eventual unity.

Let us now briefly look at the two principal instruments of Afro-Arab co-operation.

The Arab League

Some writers have credited the British with the idea of the Arab League. They say that in 1944, as a result of encouragement by the British Government, discussions took place between Egypt and a number of other Arab States about the possibility of establishing an Arab League. Some Arab scholars argue that Egypt and other co-founders of the Arab League acted on their own initiative. With or without encouragement by the British Government, the League of Arab States was formed in 1945 to advance Arab interests and reduce foreign intervention in the region. The founder members were Egypt, Iraq, Lebanon, Saudi Arabia, Syria and Transjordan and the Arab community of Palestine. Other Arab States joined after becoming independent. Now all Arab states from Morocco to the Gulf are members of the League. The new members are Mauritania who joined in December 1973,and Somalia in February 1974. For the purpose of membership of the League, Palestine is considered to be an independent State.

There are at the moment 20 member-States. The Secretariat is headed by the Secretary-General and has departments for economic, political, legal, cultural, social and labour affairs and for petroleum, finance, Palestine, health, press and information, communications and protocol. It also has specialized agencies and bureaux.

In recent years economic matters have been placed on the priority list. A Council for Arab Economic Unity was established in June 1964 with five members: Jordan, Iraq, Egypt, Syria and Kuwait. Yemen-Sanaa and Sudan joined later. The Council is like a customs union. Its aims include the removal of internal tariffs, the establishment of common external tariffs, freedom of movement of labour and capital and the adoption of common economic policies. In many respects the council operates like the European Economic Community. By 1971 tariffs on agricultural products had been abolished, and free movement of industrial products between member-States achieved. In April 1976 the Arab States set up their own Monetary Fund. They will be the main contributors, and the Fund will have its own Special Drawing Rights. The money will be used to develop industries in the Arab States — making the region less dependent on oil.

Critics have said that although the Arab World is united by common culture and religion and common heritage there are great disparities in size, economic levels, traditions and political ideology. These differences have hampered the work of the League to a certain extent. Because of them the original idea supported by Iraq of organic unity has been replaced by the concept of a loose grouping of sovereign states under the leadership of Egypt. In this regard the role of the League has been reduced to that of a consultative body whose resolutions are nothing more than recommendations which must be referred to individual member-States for approval. This is one area in which reform is probably necessary.

The OAU

The Organization of African Unity was formed after a summit meeting in Addis Ababa in 1963 which managed to bring together two separate groups in Africa: the 'Casablanca group' of progressive states who favoured an African federation and the 'Monrovia group' of conservatives who wanted no more than a loose association. The aims and purposes agreed on in Addis Ababa included the promotion of unity and solidarity among African States, the defence of sovereignty, territorial integrity and independence of member-States, and the eradication of all forms of colonialism.

The Assembly of Heads of State of the OAU meets at least once every year, while the Council of Ministers meets at least twice a year. There are specialized commissions covering mediation, conciliation and arbitration between States, as well as for economic and social affairs, education, culture and defence. The Liberation Committee provides financial and military aid to nationalist movements in colonial and minority-ruled countries. The OAU's permanent headquarters in Addis Ababa is managed by a Secretary-General, Assistant Secretary-Generals and a permanent staff working in departments covering political, legal, economic, social and cultural matters.

CO-ORDINATION

The Council of Ministers of the OAU, meeting in its twenty-fourth Ordinary Session in Addis Ababa, Ethiopia, from 13 to 21 February 1975, devoted the first four days to matters relating to Afro-Arab co-operation. It emerged that the OAU saw Afro-Arab solidarity as a necessity. Bearing in mind the need to consolidate the necessary conditions for Afro-Arab co-operation, the Council of Ministers set up a Committee of twelve countries (Cameroon, Tanzania, Uganda, Mali, Botswana, Zaire, Sudan, Algeria, Senegal, Sierra Leone, Burundi and Egypt) as a Co-ordinating Committee for Afro-Arab co-operation. It was given the task of exploring new horizons in this field, and of making specific recommendations to the first Afro-Arab Summit.

After the Cairo Summit the same Committee became responsible for the implementation of the decisions and resolutions of the Heads of State and Government. The Administrative Secretary-General was requested to set up within his Secretariat a unit entrusted with the responsibility of servicing the work of the Committee of Twelve.

The second body created to ensure the realization of Afro-Arab co-operation was the Orientation Committee, composed of Ministers from the Committee of Twelve of the Arab League and the Committee of Twelve of the OAU together with both Secretary-Generals. The Committee was given specific terms of reference. It was to supervise the process of co-operation and to follow up development in various related fields. It was to examine and direct co-operation towards the political, cultural, social, technical, and economic objectives assigned to it as well as approve and implement the co-operation programme.

The third group consists of seven separate study groups, which cover: Industrialization; Trade; Infrastructure and Telecommunications; Financial Co-operation; Cultural, Social Affairs and Information; Agricultural and Rural Development; Co-operation and Technology. Each study group may submit any appropriate proposals within its competence, to the two (Arab and African) Chairmen, especially with regard to the selection and implementation of projects, with due consideration to the instructions issued by the Orientation Committee. To allow for specialization within the group, each group may, after consultation with the two Chairmen, set up specialized panels to undertake any specific assignment within its competence. In this regard each study group is allowed to hire the services of specialists from the public or private sectors. The study groups will submit their proposals and recommendations to the Orientation Committee for approval before implementing them.

The three bodies, the Orientation Committee, the Study Groups and the Co-ordinating Committee are expected to do the ground-work for Afro-Arab Summits, which will be held, in principle, every three years.

CHAPTER THREE

ECONOMIC DEVELOPMENT IN THE ARAB WORLD

Many demands have been made on the financial resources of the Arab oil-exporting countries both by developed and developing nations. Italy for example has attracted Arab dollars for her motor industry, which has been adversely affected both by the recent global recession and by frequent strikes. American arms manufacturers have found a ready market for some of their latest weapons in certain Arab countries. Developing nations have themselves appealed for financial help to the Arab oil-exporting community, either collectively as countries of the Third World, or independently, as member-States of the OAU or other bodies. In this section we discuss some of the ways in which the additional oil revenue is being used.

A word about Iran is in order at this point: Saudi Arabia and Iran are the two giants in the Middle East. A cartel of these two countries would have a profound impact on all petroleum products in the international market. But Iran is not strictly an integral part of the Arab World. However, since most of the statistics available on the Arab oil-exporting countries are about Middle East oil revenues including those of Iran, it is difficult to cut out all reference to that country.

Despite the massive oil revenues, now in excess of $100 billion a year, of the main Middle Eastern oil-producing countries, it is probably not an exaggeration to say that if all the plans which are on the books of these countries were to be fulfilled the current surpluses which some of them have would be turned into deficits. Those who are prone to exaggerate the revenue surpluses fail to take into account the domestic requirements of the countries concerned. The key here lies in the spending capacity of the oil-producing countries, and this has often been either ignored or misunderstood.

The spending capacity of a country is closely related to its infrastructure base, the size of its territory, the size of its population and their consumer habits. Broadly speaking the countries under review can be classified under three headings:

those with large territories and large populations, i.e. Algeria and Iraq; those with large territories and relatively small populations: Saudi Arabia, Libya and Oman; and those with small territories and small populations: the Emirates (city-states) of the Gulf, Abu Dhabi, Dubai, Kuwait and Qatar.

Countries with large territories and sizeable populations require considerable expenditure to meet their development needs. The areas in question are capable of producing a variety of agricultural products and minerals, but all these require much greater capital expenditure than they have hitherto been able to employ. By definition, large territorial areas need a great deal of capital for the development of roads, railways, schools, hospitals, administrative centres, air and road transport and other communications required by a modern State. In a developing country this often literally means starting from scratch.

In a country like Algeria, with a population of 16.5 million which is estimated to grow to about 18 million by 1980, the need for more capital investment cannot be overemphasized. In 1970 the hydrocarbon sector accounted for 15 per cent of the GDP; by 1974 it made up about 40 per cent of a GDP which had increased by over 100 per cent; State revenue in 1975 amounted to about $4,000 million. This figure was 55 per cent higher than the previous year and about 70 per cent of it is derived from oil and natural gas. As a result of huge increases in expenditure on social services, however, and the ambitious development programme which is to be completed within the present decade, Algeria is likely to continue running deficits. The balance of payments has shown a deficit since 1969, and trade allocation in 1975 for exports of $4,200 million (90 per cent from energy products) was outstripped by imports of $5,600 million.

Iraq, with a smaller population of about 11 million, has had a buoyant economy since 1969. Between 1965 and 1969 oil revenue represented between 30 and 40 per cent of Iraq's GNP. Currently it accounts for about 60 per cent and constitutes 95 per cent of export revenue. The country's trade balance has been favourable for the last seven years but the need for directly productive investment in Iraq is clearly immense. Over the next five years the Government is expected to be spending \$8.5-\$10.5 billion on improvements in agriculture, whilst industrial output should rise from 5 per cent to 10 per cent of the GDP during the same period. Within the next decade therefore, Iraq, like Algeria, is capable of producing an expenditure explosion of the same order as her revenue explosion.

The next category consists of countries with large territories and relatively small populations. These include Saudi Arabia, Libya and Oman. To give some idea of the size of these countries: Arabia is ten times the size of Britain but has a population of only about 6 million; Libya has almost 2.5 million and Oman around 750,000. In all these countries, despite the huge proportion of desert, there are numerous areas in which revenue can be invested. In Saudi Arabia, the \$200 million which has already been spent on exploration has yielded good results. They have discovered several deposits of minerals such as iron and copper and other metals of commercial value. These discoveries have led the Saudi Arabian Government to earmark several billion dollars for further mineral explorations. Libya, rated as the poorest country in the world by the World Bank in 1954 before the discovery of oil, now has ambitious projects underway to develop both agriculture and industry. The latest development plan for 1976-80 has been allocated a budget of \$21 billion, 35 per cent of which is to go into these two sectors.

Oman has used most of her development budget over the past few years on non-productive capital investment. In the next five years however, she hopes to double agricultural production. On 1977's development budget is also expected to appear a \$150 million copper-production project which is to be undertaken in collaboration with a Canadian company.

Each of the three countries thus appears to have ambitious development plans and to have hired competent technicians from overseas to help realize them. In an attempt to be self-sufficient however, some of these countries have embarked on economic schemes which are neither economically sound nor viable propositions. For example one country in this group has embarked on a \$5 million project to produce less than

6,000 tons of vegetables a year. This project is certainly not viable and can only be maintained at such a high cost as long as oil continues to flow and the price continues to be remunerative to the producer.

Countries in this category are likely to have a revenue surplus which they can invest in countries of the Third World, including Africa. Although the countries generally have good and well-costed plans it is unlikely that they will complete them on schedule. Many of the projects cost $1,000 million or more each; such projects require trained manpower, and scarce, specialized capital equipment, and involve complicated tender procedures. These problems are very likely to delay the completion of the projects so that the budget funds will not be utilized within the estimated period, hence the expected revenue surplus. Another reason why the projects are not likely to be completed within a reasonable period is that the infrastructure base is not sufficiently developed to cope with the increased needs of the countries concerned. Saudi Arabia and Oman have both recognized this constraint and have taken appropriate steps to improve the situation. In Saudi Arabia, under the Second Plan, $43 billion has been allocated to infrastructure projects, $4 billion of this to be spent on road building. Oman has already undertaken a number of infrastructure projects and is now in the process of completing basic arterial roads linking the north and south of the country.

Countries in category three are those with small territories and small populations. These include the 'City State' Emirates of the Gulf, Abu Dhabi, Dubai, Kuwait and Qatar (UAE). These have smaller investment needs and opportunities partly because of their limited size and population and partly because of the lack in some cases of an adequate infrastructural base. Within these countries there are, however, pressures to improve transport, communications and other essential services. In Abu Dhabi the bulk of development spending ($600 million in 1976) has been going on infrastruature; Qatar is spending large sums on broadening the base of her economy: in the 1976 budget $370 million was set aside for the development of heavy industry. Agriculture too is being massively funded.

Throughout the Arab oil-producing world the following trend is apparent, which we can illustrate by taking Oman as an example. In 1971 oil revenues in Oman were only 23 per cent of those of 1974; in 1971 the country enjoyed both balance of payments and budgetary surpluses. In 1974 however, Oman had a balance of payments and budgetary deficit, since both imports and internal current and capital expenditure substantially increased. Between 1971 and 1974 the number of civil servants rose by about 400%, and development expenditure went up by 50%. What happened in Oman has happened elsewhere: nearly all the countries under consideration have spent large sums of money on development projects of various kinds, and these are taking up a large proportion of their budget surpluses.

In addition to rising domestic expenditure, the mounting cold war with Israel has meant that Arab defence-spending has increased substantially. Defence-spending figures are often not readily available, but in 1975 it would appear that Saudi Arabia spent in the region of $6,000 million on defence, Algeria $250 million, Kuwait $120 million. As weapons increase in sophistication they also become more costly, and this is another factor which has affected Arab defence budgets as much as those of any other country.

One of the problems faced by Arab oil-producing states wishing to industrialize is that although they all have the raw materials for petrochemical and allied industries, only about half of them have much else on which to build manufacturing activities. In 1975 Iran, which has a sizeable population, had to recruit textile workers of various grade from Britain. Iraq and Algeria, though they have huge populations, are handicapped by the absence of skilled labour. It could be argued that with the millions and millions of dollars owned by Arab States they should be able to recruit skilled manpower from all corners of the world. This is exactly what the oil States are trying to do — but it should be appreciated that immigrant or hired expatriate skilled labour is not always *easy* to recruit. This type of worker usually belongs to the middle class in his home country and is generally well-educated. He is likely to be concerned about the welfare of his children and would require, apart from high emoluments, benefits such as good educational and medical facilities, comfortable accommodation to compensate for the adverse climate of most arid lands, and general good working conditions.

The problem of the shortage of skilled labour in Arab oil-producing countries is compounded by the fact that, being thinly-populated, they tend to go for capital-intensive rather than labour-intensive industries. Capital-intensive industries require, in addition to specialized skills, high technology, imported plant; and the availability of this is restricted by the production capacity of the manufacturing country.

The presence of foreign skilled labour requiring additional social benefits has also meant that the demand for education and medical facilities has begun to rise amongst nationals of the oil-producing countries. Nationals and foreigners alike have come to expect that employers will provide them with free accommodation, water, electricity etc., despite the fact that the cost of all these services has risen appreciably.

A final point is that custom and tradition play a large and sometimes expensive part in Arab life. The oil-rich Arab States for example subsidize the cost of pilgrimages to Mecca. Moslems from Africa and Asia who want to go to Mecca to pray are advised to go in large numbers from one area so that the rich Arab Moslem states will subsidize the cost of their travel. Traditional cultural values and social customs remain strong. It is a fact that lavish expenditure on social welfare is common to all Islamic countries. Personal obligations and allegiances are more important than contractual relationships, and the extended family system, for example, can at times be very costly.

We have tried to bring out in this section some of the ways in which Arab oil-producing countries are using their oil revenues at the present time. What emerges is that their domestic requirements are such that most of them are unlikely to have large surpluses to distribute in aid to developing countries. Clearly the emphasis of Afro-Arab economic co-operation should be not on aid but on commercial relations based on the exchange of goods and services.

ARAB OIL RESERVES

Oil revenues are the mainstay of the economies of most of the Arab oil-producing countries. Inevitably since the oil resources are limited the question of how long these are going to last is critical. Clearly this depends very largely on present and future production levels. These in turn are related on the one hand to world demand for oil as a source of energy and on the other to political decisions, taken by OPEC or by individual oil-producing States, to conserve their most valuable asset.

As far as the world demand for oil is concerned, the post-war period presents a picture of rapid growth both in energy production and energy consumption. During this time coal, for a number of reasons, decreased in importance as a source of energy, while oil production expanded. A study of the relevant figures indicates that the share of liquid fuel in total energy production increased from 29.8% in 1950 to 49.2% in 1974, whereas the share of solid fuel decreased from 59.3% in 1950 to 29% in 1974. Oil came to be used not only as a primary energy source but also in numerous other sectors as the base for petrochemicals, fertilizers and many pharmaceutical products.

During most of the period since 1945 the major oil companies controlled the level of oil production so that it kept pace with consumer demand. Between 1950 and 1974 the average annual growth in energy production was similar to that of energy consumption, i.e. about 5%. Industrial expansion in particular has been marked by an increase in energy consumption. Until recently industrialized countries have maintained a steady rise in economic growth and their overall energy requirements have shown a corresponding increase. At all times developed countries have consumed a far greater proportion of the total world energy production than the others. This can be brought out by considering the fact that for over a quarter of a century the per capita energy consumption in the developed countries has been three times that of the world average. If we compare this with the developing countries alone, then this figure rises to sixteen times. Needless to say the past consumption of the developing countries reflects their underdevelopment.

It was against this background that the oil-producing countries decided to raise their prices in 1973. They argued that since the Second World War oil prices had been kept artificially low, in spite of the increase in importance of oil as a source of world energy. The oil industry was controlled by international companies whose interests were not those of the oil-producing countries. The price rises imposed by OPEC were designed both to put a stop to the exploitation suffered by the oil-producing nations and to check world demand for oil in an effort to slow down the rate at which resources would be depleted.

If we consider the fact that prior to 1973 oil was articially under-priced by several dollars per barrel, it can be seen that for many years the developing world has been financing the economies of the developed countries to the tune of hundreds of billions of dollars. It is for this reason that, in spite of the adverse effects of the oil-price increases on the economies of the Third World countries, some of them actually supported the price rises in the hope that other commodities produced by developing countries would follow the same trend. Such commodities might include manganese, cobalt, nickel or bauxite. For the moment, however, oil producers are alone in successfully exerting pressure. The prices of other commodities exported to industrialized countries from the Third World are still relatively depressed.

If we look at the effects of the 1973 decision on the world energy picture we find that the demand for oil in the major consumer states fell in the following year by about 10%. Between 1977 and 1985 the increase in demand is not likely to be substantial. It is estimated that it would go from 47.6 million barrels a day in 1973 to 52.2 million barrels a day in 1980 and 57.5 million barrels a day in 1985. If these assumptions are proved correct the oil consumption in the United States, Europe and Japan, which are the main industrial areas, will be as shown in Table I.

These estimates are lower than earlier projections which were made before the increase in the price of oil in 1973. At that time it was estimated that demand would be 74 million barrels a day in 1980, and as much as 100 million barrels a day

TABLE I

Million barrels a day	1973	1980	1985
United States	16.8	18.0	19.5
Europe	15.2	15.4	18.0
Japan	5.4	6.6	7.9

in 1985. The decline in the demand can be explained by the recent slowing down of the growth rates of the industrialized countries and by the measures which have already been taken to reduce their dependence upon oil.

This will become clearer if we look at the three major consumer areas in turn.

1. The United States

Future supply and demand of energy in the United States will depend on the following major factors:

— Government policies on energy conservation, domestic resource development, fuel substitutes and foreign energy supplies.

— Structural changes underway in the US economy since the oil-price increases and production cuts of 1973; the magnitude and timing of these changes is an area of considerable uncertainty.

— Domestic economic framework with particular regard to parameters such as capital formation, sectoral cash flow and the like.

The United States probably more than any other Western country has a developed framework within which to analyse the impact of these and other factors upon the country's energy situation. A good deal of the relevant information is available in the National Energy Outlook which was released in March 1976. These studies provide the following figures.

Energy investment: Energy investments in the United States will be about $580 billion (in 1975 dollars) in the next ten years. This investment is about 30% of fixed business investment. However, in certain sectors such as utilities, a large demand will be placed on the capital markets. Oil, gas, and electrical utility capital spending will almost double in the next ten years. The largest portion of energy investment will be on electricity in an effort to move away from oil to some alternative source of power. This could account for 47% of the total. Coal investment could increase to $18 billion. This is only 3% of the overall sum but represents a 200% increase on the 1964-74 figure of $6 billion.

Future projections: Imports will continue to increase for the next few years, but will decline significantly when Alaskan production begins and again when other energy sources become available. During the next ten years, as a result of higher prices alone, energy demand will grow much more slowly than it has done in the past, even if economic expansion is maintained. Energy demand grew at a rate of 3.6% in the 20 years before the 1973 embargo, and in 1975 the United States consumed about 73 quadrillion BTUs (quads). Electricity consumption grew at twice the rate of other forms of energy. With current oil prices, coupled with US government policies relating to energy conservation, the total primary energy demand should be 98.9 quads in 1985. Electricity requirements will still grow about twice as fast as the overall demand for energy but at a reduced level of 5.4% per year. Consumers will gradually shift from oil and gas to coal and nuclear energy.

2. Japan

Japan is much more dependent that either the United States or the countries of the EEC on oil imports since her own energy resources are virtually non-existent. When the oil-price rises hit the industrialized world in 1973 the Japanese set themselves the task of considerably reducing their dependence upon oil over the coming decade. Target demand figures were set to be attained by the co-operative efforts of Government, industrialists and domestic consumers. The Energy Plan was based on the adoption of policies to conserve energy and to develop alternative sources. The overall aim was to achieve a stable energy situation in the light of supply constraints. If the plan's objectives are attained, this would mean an annual GNP growth rate in real terms of about 6.6% over the period 1975-1985. The authors of the plan claim that Japan's dependence on imported petroleum would decline from 77% in fiscal year 1973 to 63% by fiscal year 1985. They nevertheless have the honesty to admit that, in spite of the efforts being made to discover alternative sources of energy, Japan, like other industrialized countries, will for the next ten to fifteen years have to depend on oil imports to maintain her current level of production.

3. The EEC

A representative of the European Economic Community said at the Paris Conference in September 1976 that the Community considers it essential to make further efforts to husband the world's limited energy resources. Community policy has for some time been aimed at reducing the calls made on the resources of the Third World by developing fresh energy sources within the EEC itself. The policy is also aimed at achieving a more rational, less wasteful use of energy in an effort to lessen overall demand.

In the period 1963-1973 the gross internal consumption of energy in the Community increased by an average of 4.5% per annum. In 1963 solid fuel supplied 53% of energy requirements. In time petroleum products came to displace coal and, by 1973 they covered 59% of the total demand. Recently, increases in supplies of natural gas have caused it to displace coal, and to some extent oil too, still further, and by 1975 natural gas accounted for 17% of the Community's consumption.

It will take several years for the Community to feel the full effects of the energy policy it has embarked upon. The delay will be due to the fact that there are a number of constraints which prevent rapid achievement of its objectives. These include:

— the flexibility of consumption patterns which can only be changed with time and under certain conditions;
— the heavy investment needed to develop the production of substitute energy forms.

In many respects the Community's plan has similar

constraints to that of the Japanese. The evolution of energy demand depends upon many factors including the rate of economic growth and relative energy prices.

The Community's energy forecast up to 1985 is not comforting to European energy consumers. By 1985 it is unlikely that new energy sources will be able to play a significant role in meeting the Community's energy requirements. There will thus be a reliance on solid fuels and nuclear energy. In spite of these constraints the Community will continue its efforts to develop domestic sources and to ensure that new energy sources make a contribution to the energy supply as soon as possible. Allowing for all the uncertainties inherent both in production and in exploration, the Community's own production of oil and natural gas will be, between 1980 and 1985: natural gas 150-165 million t.o.e. (tons of oil equivalent); crude oil 110-160 million t.o.e.

Estimates based on natural gas import contracts, both existing and under negotiation, suggest that the Community will require 60 million t.o.e. from outside in 1980 and 95 million t.o.e. in 1985. Oil imports may be between 365 million t.o.e. and 510 million t.o.e. in 1980, and 360 million t.o.e. and 610 million t.o.e. in 1985. The Community's energy experts are reluctant to forecast energy requirements for the period 1985-1990. They say that there are no reliable means of doing this. Even small variations in the trend of economic growth or in the availability of non-hydro-carbon resources would have a significant impact on the rate and nature of energy consumption in 1980 and 1985. These uncertainties have even greater effect on attempts to foresee conditions in 1990 or later.

WORLD ENERGY OUTLOOK AND PROPOSALS FOR POSITIVE INTERDEPENDENCE

The overall picture in all the areas considered is similar in that efforts are being made to check excessive energy consumption and to develop alternative fuel sources. This is likely to have the additional advantage of decreasing the incidence of pollution in the industrialized countries. In spite of the measures which have been taken however, the major oil-consuming nations will almost certainly remain heavily dependent on oil for at least the next decade. The projected consumption figures were revised after 1973 in the light of the price rises and the energy policies which were then undertaken. But even these revised figures suggest that present production levels will have to be increased if demand is to be met.

Because of the impetus given to exploration and prospecting by the price increases of 1973, it may be possible to raise production in the non-OPEC countries by 1980 to over 20 million barrels a day. The likely sources are Alaska, (which will probably produce 2 million b/d) and United States production south of the forty-ninth parallel (which could be maintained near the 1973 level of 11 million *b/d* if the US Federal Government were to release the reservoirs earmarked for the US navy in wartime). It is also expected that the UK sector of the North Sea will be producing 2 to 3 million *b/d*, and that Canada will maintain her output of 2 million *b/d*. The Middle East as a region is expected to raise its output from 21 million to 23 million barrels a day.

The Middle East is capable of increasing its output to an even higher figure than the present estimates. At the end of 1973 the proven reserves of the Persian Gulf were 350 billion barrels, and this figure was almost two-thirds of the non-communist world total. The breakdown shows Saudi Arabia with 148 billion barrels, Kuwait and Iran 65 billion barrels each, Iraq 30 billion barrels, Abu Dhabi 29 billion barrels, the Kuwait/Saudi Arabia partitioned zone 10 billion barrels, Qatar 7 billion barrels, and in Oman, Dubai, Sharjah and Bahrain combined 6 billion barrels. Libya, Algeria and Tunisia contain a further 50 billion barrels.

Raising their output becomes attractive to the Middle East countries only if two conditions are met: the first being that buyers pay a reasonable price for oil, and the second, that Western countries provide the necessary protection and safeguards required by Arab investors. As things stand, cash surpluses will be accumulated by oil-exporting developing countries not by design but by compulsion, compulsion to meet the energy requirements of the world community, mainly the industrialized countries themselves. Having parted with their depleting resources in quantities disproportionate to their immediate needs, oil-exporting countries justifiably expect that the assets they have been acquiring in exchange for their oil will get the full protection of the most developed governments and that the restrictions on such assets will be removed. Basically the assets we are referring to consist of demand and time deposits with the banks and bankers' acceptances; debit instruments of government, government agencies and instrumentalities and public corporations; debit instruments of companies and corporations in the private sector; common stock and other equity investment and real estate. These assets have been subjected to the following risks: continuing erosion of capital as a result of inflation; frequent capital loss accruing from external depreciations of currencies caused by floating rates; restriction on movement of capital imposed by national authorities from time to time; implication of control of the euro-currency market; and working taxes on incomes or gain or investment of sovereign funds.

For the purpose of investing, the Arab investor should be accorded similar privileges and obligations to any other investor in the capital market. The discriminatory barriers which are often placed by national authorities to check capital flows of developing countries should be dispensed with. These barriers include: nonpayment of interest to non-residents on bank deposits; the ineligibility for holding certain popular debit instruments; official permission required for purchase and sale of domestic debit instruments.

These appeals are made in full knowledge of the fact that the countries in question are sovereign states which are free to act in accordance with their national laws and are subject to the dictates of their national interests. As Chancellor Schmidt of the Federal Republic of Germany told foreign socialist delegates who had come to attend the German Socialist Party Convention — they should take care not to ask the German government to pursue policies unattractive to the German electorate, else on their next visit they would not find them in power. However, we are not asking the countries concerned to do the impossible; we are merely asking them that in their dealings with the developing countries they should not be discriminatory.

TABLE II

Millions barrels a day	1973	1974	1980
Bahrain	0.06	0.06	0.06
Sharjah	0.0	0.1	0.2
Oman	0.3	0.3	0.4
Dubai	0.3	0.3	0.3
Qatar	0.6	0.5	0.5
Partitioned Zone	0.5	0.5	0.5
Kuwait	2.8	2.3	1.7
Abu Dhabi	1.3	1.3	1.5
Iraq	2.0	1.9	2.3
Iran	5.9	6.1	5.8
Saudi Arabia	7.3	8.2	9.5
TOTAL:	21.06	21.56	22.76

By the same token the Arab investor should not discriminate against the African economies. He should not place all his eggs in one basket, namely the Western world. The amount of $1.5 billion the Arab countries have pledged to invest in Africa should be the minimum amount of financial assistance to Africa. Some experts on Arab funds are of the opinion that $2 billion is the peak of Arab aid to Africa between 1977 and 1980 because very few Arab countries (such as Kuwait and Dubai) will have substantial surpluses, while others who have in the past provided half the group's aid will reduce it as their imports rise to fulfil their expanding development requirements. This is perfectly correct; but it is equally true to say that if the Middle East countries were given incentives to increase their oil production they could also continue to contribute substantial amounts to the economic development plans of the other countries of the Third World.

If the Middle East oil-producers are accorded the necessary incentives stated in this chapter it ought to be worthwhile for them to produce as much oil as the oil-importing countries require. If this happens we can reasonably forecast a breakdown of the Middle Eastern countries' production levels in 1980 as shown in Table II. Such production levels would ensure a certain harmony in energy distribution throughout the world, and would be sufficient to keep development in the Arab world on an even keel. But will they also facilitate a steady growth in Afro-Arab co-operation?

CHAPTER FOUR

ECONOMIC DEVELOPMENT IN AFRICA

In an unprecedented upsurge of dedication towards jointly solving their economic problems, the African Economic Ministers have recently been holding regular meetings to try and work out a common strategy to improve the economic situation in Africa. They have declared themselves in favour of improving intra-African co-operation, economic relations and the exchange of goods and services among African States, and of increasing co-operation between Africa and the other countries of the Third World.

A meeting held in February-March 1977 in Kinshasa, under the auspices of the United Nations Economic Commission for Africa (ECA), clearly spelled out the fundamental problems and the hopes for improvement. Varying ideals were put forward. It was suggested that Africa's strategy should be based on:

1. developing Africa's enormous economic potential;
2. promoting the exchange of goods and services among African countries;
3. economic integration at a pan-African level to ensure self-sufficiency for Africa's economies;
4. Africa holding in its hands all the elements required for self-sufficiency and survival, while remaining open to trade relations with the industrialized world, so as to contribute to the establishment of the New International Economic Order — as long as the industrialized countries agree to make the necessary sacrifices.

The delegates at Kinshasa noted with alarm that the development and revival of the economies of the rich countries have not benefitted Africa in recent years. The interdependence between Africa and the industrialized countries often leads to imbalance which severely affects the African countries. The damaging repercussions of inflation in the industrialized countries on the Third World economies in recent months and years are adequate proof of the economic difficulties of such interdependence. Economic conditions are continuing to deteriorate throughout most of the continent, but Africa can no longer allow itself to accept such a slow pace of development as in the past fifteen or more years of political independence. Even if the world economic order were basically re-organized Africa could benefit from it only by re-organizing its own structures at national, sub-regional and regional levels.

The Economic Commission for Africa has done valuable research on the state of the African economy. In general terms, its reports dramatically illustrate how poorly Africa has been performing in the last decade-and-a-half and how dim the prospects are for the rest of this century, unless the present international economic system changes and the African Governments themselves rethink their economic policies.

The ECA summarised the main features of the African economy during 1960-75 as follows:

Firstly, because of the excessive external dependence of the African economy, development has been substantially affected by cyclical fluctuations in the economies of the industrialized countries, particularly OECD member countries, which form the major export markets for African countries. This dependence is so pervasive that the upswings and downswings in the industrialized market economies affect the values of African exports, the terms of trade, the cost and value of imports, the level of inflation, and, ultimately, the trends and levels of Gross Domestic Product.

Secondly, for the period between 1960 and 1975 Africa north of the Zambezi achieved an average annual growth rate of only 4.9 per cent per annum. During the first United Nations Development Decade, 1960-1970, the average was 5 per cent per annum, but during the first half of the Second Development Decade the average fell to 4.5 per cent.

Thirdly, inflation accelerated substantially in the later part of the 1960s and the first half of the 1970s. In consequence of the excessive external dependence of the African economy, a good part of the inflation was imported. Inflation, coupled with the recession, led to a sharp fall in the value of export commodities and a steep rise in the value of imports seriously affecting government revenue from export and import duties.

Partly in consequence, wages and salaries were substantially increased in many countries and attempts were made to subsidize essential consumer goods, with attendant large increases in public expenditure. Many African Governments had to resort to deficit financing which inevitably aggravated the inflationary pressure.

Fourthly, the debt burden of many African States is growing rapidly. During the past 15 years more and more African States have unfortunately had to learn to live with this phenomenon. The region's share in the debt burden rose from US$ 7 billion in 1965 to more than US$ 28 billion in 1974. As a result, outlays for interest and amortization charges represent a rapidly growing percentage of total export earnings, amounting to as much as 30 per cent for some African countries in contrast to the World Bank's 10 per cent ceiling. This situation is aggravated by the fact that for a number of countries the foreign currencies in which some of their debt obligations are denominated have appreciated, thus resulting in big increases in the cost of debt servicing. Consequently, many African countries have had no option other than to borrow on a short-term basis or run down their meagre reserves or do both. Unfortunately on this vital issue of the crippling debt burden no meaningful resolution could be adopted at the fourth session of UNCTAD. And what is even worse, with respect to other related issues such as the provision of an adequate flow of development finance and the reform of the international monetary system, UNCTAD IV could not even bring itself to adopt any resolution at all.

Fifthly, and perhaps most seriously, growth in the agricultural production sector — on which over four-fifths of Africa's entire population depends and which for most countries is the main source of foreign exchange earnings and public revenue — is slow. The disappointing performance of the agricultural sector, accentuated by drought conditions in the early 1970s, also led to increased food imports at high prices, thus worsening the precarious balance-of-payments position of most countries.

Thus, economic performance in Africa has fallen substantially below the targets set in the *Strategy for the Second United*

Nations Development Decade. The target annual growth in GDP at constant prices set in the *Strategy* is 6 per cent; about 7 per cent for imports and exports; half a percentage point rise yearly in the rate of gross domestic savings to the gross product; 4 per cent for agriculture; and 8 per cent for manufacturing. African performance fell below the various targets except in imports where it accelerated to 10 per cent yearly between 1970 and 1975 from 4.4 per cent per annum during the period 1960 to 1970, as against the deceleration in export growth to 2.8 per cent yearly during the period 1970 to 1975 from 7.8 per cent per annum during the First Development Decade.

In other words, there has been no marked improvement in most African economies since 1960. The African economy today still exhibits all the characteristics of underdevelopment. And compared with the other regions of the developing world, Africa has fared worst. The average annual rates of growth of the GDP were substantially higher in Latin America, the Middle East, East and South-East Asia and the Pacific than they have been in Africa. Only in South Asia (the Indian subcontinent and Burma) were the growth rates lower than those of Africa. Similarly, the performances in both the agricultural and manufacturing sectors were better in the other Third World regions, which have managed to achieve a higher annual rate of increase in the manufacturing industry than the target rate of 8 per cent per annum of the Second Development Decade. The rates of increase in food production in these regions were also generally above the rates of increase in their population.

In the words of the ECA Executive Secretary, Dr Adebayo Adedeji:

> 'Africa, more than the other Third World regions, is faced with a development crisis of great portent. In spite of the region's ample natural resources, of a favourable population to natural resources ratio, in spite of the generous and even indiscriminating incentives for foreign private enterprise, in spite of our participation in numerous conferences both regional and inter-regional, and in spite of our adherence to

> orthodox theories and prescriptions — in spite of all these, neither high rates of growth nor of diversification nor an increasing measure of self-reliance and dynamism seems to be within our reach.'

But Dr Adedeji is still hopeful that 'there lies within the power of member-States means of alleviating the debt burden and of building into the socio-economic system capabilities for escaping from this grave situation.'

The overall picture of the economic performance of Africa during the past decade-and-a-half conceals large differences among the different sub-regions and groups of countries. The ECA has classified African countries into five economic categories. There is, first, the group of major oil-exporters — Algeria, Gabon, Libya and Nigeria. The non-oil-exporting countries are classified into four groups on the basis of *per capita* incomes: US$300-400, US$200-300, US$100-200, and below US$100. Of the 41 non-oil-exporting countries on which data are available, five countries — Congo, Ivory Coast, Sao Tome and Principe, Tunisia and Zambia — belong to the first *per capita* income category (US$300-400); 11 countries — Cape Verde, Egypt, Equatorial Guinea, Ghana, Guinea-Bissau, Liberia, Mauritius, Morocco, Mozambique, Senegal,and Swaziland — belong to the second category (US$200-300); another set of 11 countries — Botswana, Cameroon, Central African Empire, The Gambia, Kenya, Madagascar, Mauritania, Sierra Leone, Sudan, Togo and Uganda — belong to the US$100-200 income range group. The last group of below US$100 *per capita* income consists of 14 countries: these are Benin, Burundi, Chad, Ethiopia, Guinea, Lesotho, Malawi, Mali, the Niger, Rwanda, Somalia, the United Republic of Tanzania, the Upper Volta and Zaire. The varying performance of these five groups of countries is revealing (see Table III). Whereas the four major oil-exporting countries and the five countries within the *per capita* income range of between US$300-400 achieved an average growth rate of 6.9 and 5.8 per cent per annum respectively between 1960 and 1975, the 14 countries whose *per capita* income is below US$100 achieved only 2.6 per cent growth rate per annum. In other words, this latter group of countries achieved *no growth at all* on a *per capita* basis during the 15 year period. Indeed, when due account has been taken of population growth in these countries, it will be clear that their economies have been declining. The 22 countries in the *per capita* income ranges of between US$100 and US$300 achieved an average growth of 4.1 per cent per annum with 1.4 per cent per annum increase in *per capita* income.

TABLE III

Annual average growth in Real GDP
(in percentages)

Countries by income categories	1960-1970	1970-1975
Major oil exporters	6.9	7.0
Non-oil-exporting countries		
Between US$300-400 *per capita*	6.5	4.5
Between US$200-300 *per capita*	3.5	5.0
Between US$100-200 *per capita*	4.3	3.1
Below US$100 *per capita*	2.5	2.8
Total non-oil-exporting countries	4.9	3.5
Total developing Africa	5.0	4.5

Source: ECA estimates, 1977

The implications of these figures are clear and rather sombre. In only 9 African countries have the growth rates achieved during the past 15 years been such as to bring about a relatively substantial increase in real *per capita* income.

PROSPECTS

In a preliminary assessment the ECA Secretariat has attempted an extremely tentative projection of prospects for the African economy. If past trends were to persist and if there are no fundamental changes in the mix of economic policies that African Governments have pursued during the past decade-and-a-half, and if the current efforts to change the international economic system and relations fundamentally fail to yield concrete results, Africa as a whole will be, relatively, worse off than the rest of the world at the end of this century than it was in 1960. Even the overall average rate of growth in GDP of developing African countries would still fall below the target rate set under the Second Development Decade. The ECA estimates the average annual growth rate, based on the above-mentioned assumptions, to be 5.5 per cent for the rest of the century (see Table IV). Within Africa, ECA estimates reveal the prospect of even greater disparities in incomes and levels of development among the countries.

TABLE IV

Forecasts of growth in GDP to the year 2000 and the relative shares in total GDP of developing African countries classified according to defined income groups

Countries by income categories at 1970 prices	Forecast Growth rate*	Shares in total GDP of developing Africa (in percentage)			
		1975	1980	1990	2000
Major oil-exporters	7.5	34.5	37.9	45.0	52.2
Non-oil-exporting countries					
Between US$300-400 *per capita*	6.0	8.6	8.8	9.0	8.8
Between US$200-300 *per capita*	5.0	30.2	29.4	27.2	24.5
Between US$100-200 *per capita*	4.0	13.6	12.6	10.6	8.7
Below US$100 *per capita*	2.5	13.1	11.3	8.2	5.8
Total non-oil-exporting countries	4.4	65.5	62.1	55.0	47.8
Total developing Africa	5.5	100.0	100.0	100.0	100.0

*Estimates based on historical trends and policies.

Source: ECA estimates, 1977.

Dr Adedeji believes that the picture can change by, among other things, improving the terms under which licences are granted to private sector companies — whether foreign or indigenous — for the exploitation of natural resources for export. Minerals, petroleum, uranium, forest products, fishery resources are all being extracted on an increasing scale with little to show in the way of self-sustaining development. Even without producers' associations, there is still room for securing better yields in real and financial terms from what seem to be exhaustible and rapidly disappearing resources. Better legislation, improved negotiating capabilities and less one-sided agreements can contribute to the net resources picture.

The ECA has also suggested the need for re-examination of the way in which development banks are organized and the way in which they function in relation to national priorities and targets. It feels that the time has come to consider how non-banking financial institutions, commercial banks, insurance funds, etc., may contribute to the financing of national priority projects. At the regional level the ECA has urged sub-regional co-operation in the management of monetary reserves and other short-term international assets; the setting up of an intra-African Development Aid System for the purpose of concentrating scarce skills and resources; the establishment of multinational mining and industrial development banks to organize the sophisticated packages of finance for mining and multinational industries on the massive scales that are, in many cases, unavoidable today. National and sub-regional development banks, central banks and insurance companies could all contribute to the resources of these specialized banks.

Dr Adedeji favours the creation of African multinational corporations in the mining and industrial fields which could: negotiate joint ventures with foreign companies; negotiate technology agreements; organize subcontracting agreements with national companies for the supply of components for multinational enterprises; and encourage technological research and innovation, organize consultancy services and promote standardization and quality control within the sectors in which they operate. If proposals such as these were to be co-ordinated with more Afro-Arab co-operation, then the prospects for Africa begin to look much brighter than the ECA has painted them.

If Arab investment continues, but at a faster rate, there are endless possibilities for large-scale mineral and agricultural schemes that would be profitable to all concerned. The ripple effects of such redistribution of wealth will be felt throughout the Afro-Arab zone. An economic community of nations sharing their wealth equitably need not be a too distant possibility.

Rising expectations amongst the governed is a common feature among the new states of Africa. African governments are under pressure to improve the social and economic well-being of their people. This is a legitimate demand which the African governments cannot ignore despite the great difficulties they face. As rational beings, African people do not expect their governments to achieve everything in the short run; but they do expect them to lay a strong foundation for the work to be completed in the long run.

African governments are aware that in order to raise the standard of living they will have to industrialize their economies. But this cannot be attained without foreign capital which is accompanied by foreign technology. In their search for foreign investment many African governments have introduced various investment incentives, i.e. tax holidays, generous capital allowances and other fiscal measures. These efforts have often met with little success because foreign investors have either shied away from supposed political instability or have harboured fears of nationalizations and reprisals against Western business. These fears are largely unfounded. The nationalizations that have occurred in the past decade have been dictated by the need to correct the balance of wealth in the world. Now that a new order is being established Africa can provide guarantees, made with full confidence of their validity in the future, that will both satisfy investors' hopes and spread new prosperity in the region.

TRADE

An area in which there is an urgent need to develop Afro-Arab

TABLE V

Less-developed Africa's trade with the Middle East 1975*
(million US dollars)

Countries traded with	African Exports	African Imports
Algeria	98	51
Egypt	72	32
Iran	45	422
Iraq	15	242
Kuwait	13	48
Libya	69	73
Oman	2	—
Qatar	3	—
Saudi Arabia	96	310
United Arab Emirates	2	—
Bahrain	1	1
Jordan	9	2
Lebanon	31	17
Syria	8	1
North Yemen	13	1
South Yemen	18	17
Total trade with Middle East	496	1,217

* 'Africa' here excludes Algeria, Egypt, Libya, Nigeria and South Africa.

relations is that of trade. There is already the basis of strong commercial ties between the Middle Eastern oil-producers and nearly every country in Black Africa, but all too often this trade is heavily in favour of the oil-exporters. African countries like Ghana, Kenya, Ivory Coast and Tanzania are each spending over $100 million a year on Middle Eastern oil, while what they sell in return to the Middle East is still insignificant; and yet all these countries are producers and exporters of both food and minerals. It is up to these countries to re-organize their traditional trading relationships and to stimulate their own exports, as much to Africa and the Middle East as to the Western World. Tables V and VI illustrate the present imbalance in Afro-Arab trade and show how it favours the large oil-producers like Iran, Iraq and Saudi Arabia. In the years to come it is to be hoped that Africa's exports to the Middle East will expand so as to restore equilibrium.

TABLE VI

Oil-exporting countries' trade with Africa 1975*
(million US dollars)

Countries traded with	Oil-producers' Exports	Oil-producers' Imports
Algeria	1	1
Angola	36	9
Benin	5	8
Botswana	—	8
Burundi	2	6
Cameroon	4	4
Chad	—	7
Congo	59	1
Djibouti	4	6
Egypt	28	111
Ethiopia	40	35
Gabon	1	—
Ghana	100	5
Guinea	7	—
Ivory Coast	121	22
Kenya	199	20
Lesotho	—	1
Liberia	26	2
Libya	4	—
Madagascar	14	1
Malawi	3	1
Mali	1	1
Mauritania	—	3
Mauritius	26	2

Morocco	152	49
Mozambique	62	11
Namibia	—	1
Niger	12	3
Nigeria	13	1
Reunion	8	—
Rwanda	3	—
Senegal	40	4
Sierra Leone	19	—
Somalia	9	84
South Africa	235	93
Sudan	25	44
Swaziland	19	2
Tanzania	131	21
Togo	7	3
Tunisia	80	88
Uganda	n.a.	4
Upper Volta	1	—
Zaire	57	7
Zambia	68	1
Spanish Africa	5	—
Africa not specified	17	79
Total trade with Africa	1,644	752

* Algeria, Indonesia, Iran, Iraq, Kuwait, Libya, Nigeria, Oman, Qatar, Saudi Arabia, UAE, Venezuela.
n.a. = not available
Source: IMF Direction of Trade

CHAPTER FIVE

FINANCIAL INSTITUTIONS FOR AFRO-ARAB CO-OPERATION

Attempting to make a thorough inventory of the channels and institutions for Arab-African co-operation is difficult. The 1973 Arab-Israeli conflict acted as a stimulus, and since that time funds, banks and other financial institutions, set up by the Arabs for improving co-operation with Africa and with the Third World in general, have mushroomed in the Middle East.

We noted earlier that political sympathy between the Middle East and Africa has been excellent on many counts; economic co-operation on the other hand, though more valuable, was scarcely developed until 1973. Since then, efforts have been made by both parties to establish appropriate machinery for the implementation of the various programmes which have been proposed. In this chapter we shall be looking at the financial institutions involved in Afro-Arab economic co-operation, and considering what measures could be taken to make them more effective.

A major problem in this area is that existing information is scattered, and little funding is available for research. The OAU and the Arab League could begin to remedy this by making an exhaustive study enabling them to assess the total volume of Arab financial resources that have been actually transferred, or definitely committed, to non-Arab African countries over the period 1974-76, through both official and private channels. The need for such a study cannot be overemphasized. It would enable both sides of the Afro-Arab partnership to agree on changes that are needed, both in the size of financial transfers and in the administration of their institutions. Above all such a study would strengthen Afro-Arab solidarity by removing any doubts or suspicions that may exist, or could arise, concerning the resources of either side.

Afro-Arab relations can be divided broadly into those which involve bilateral agreements and those which are channelled through international agencies. Neither of these is in any absolute sense better than the other, but in general donors favour bilateral agreements, since they are able to monitor the use being made of their financial assistance. Recipients on the other hand often feel that bilateral aid is tied aid.

Projects selected for joint Afro-Arab effort should ideally be ones essential to the development of the economies of the African countries concerned. As things are, there is not always a great deal of co-ordination amongst Arab countries, so the range of projects covered is wide and often unrelated to the general economic goals established by the OAU. It is necessary for certain strategic areas to be selected for development: the serious food crisis which has been highlighted by the UN Food and Agriculture Organization should be the first priority. Africans and Arabs must jointly ensure that agriculture and related areas are developed sufficiently during the next ten to fifteen years to meet the food needs of Africa and the other Third World countries.

Another important area which needs special attention is the development of infrastructure — roads, railways, air and sea transport, communications, schools, hospitals and other essential social services. This is a much broader area than agricultural development, but adequate studies would indicate the dimensions of the problem and the key areas which could be selected for the initiation of the programme.

The creation of a solid infrastructural base is a prerequisite for the success of many other types of projects. Therefore an extensive survey of known and as yet undiscovered natural resources in the Afro-Arab world should also be undertaken. This is an essential element of any sound and realistic plan for the effective use of Afro-Arab resources.

There are two further points which need to be raised before we go on to consider existing financial institutions in more detail. The first relates to the distribution of any given flow of Arab financial resources to non-Arab African countries. Should it be based on the population distribution and relative size of the countries concerned and on their development potential, or should it be based on *need*, which means giving higher priority to the least developed and most geographically disadvantaged (e.g. landlocked) countries?

The second point is more of a recommendation than a question: Arab resources should help to stimulate regional and sub-regional co-operation within Africa by supporting projects which benefit more than one country. Here we have in mind particularly projects which bring together neighbouring African and Arab countries. We have stated elsewhere in this book that African and Arab unity is a long-term ideal and that in the short-term we should attempt to achieve Afro-Arab co-operation. What we are suggesting is that one way of strengthening Afro-Arab co-operation is the promotion of joint ventures in specific areas, such as agriculture, animal production, mining, shipping etc., in which both governments and private institutions can participate. Needless to say, only large-scale, powerful co-operation can stand up to the giant foreign-based multinationals which control important sectors of the economies of both African and Arab countries.

MULTILATERAL ARAB INSTITUTIONS

Financial assistance which is not on a bilateral basis can only be effected properly by specialized multilateral institutions. These include:

1. The Arab Bank for Economic Development in Africa (BADEA)

Because of its unique importance to Africa this bank will be discussed more fully later in this chapter. BADEA was established as a result of a decision of the Sixth Arab Summit Conference held in Algiers in November 1973. It has a total capital of $231 million, subscribed by 18 Arab governments. By March 1976 $124.5 million had been committed to the financing of development projects in 19 African countries.

It was realized at the very outset that a capital of $231 million was inadequate to meet the needs of Africa, particularly since the 41 non-Arab African countries include some of the least developed countries in the world. The Seventh Arab Summit Conference held in Rabat in October 1974 decided to increase the capital even before BADEA was operational. However, in terms of the Charter of the Bank, the decision of the Summit Conference could not be implemented until the first meeting of the BADEA Board of Governors took place in November and December 1976. As expected the Board endorsed the decision to increase the capital of the Bank.

2. Special Arab Fund for Africa (SAFA)

This is the second Arab institution which was set up almost at the same time as BADEA to provide emergency financial assistance to non-Arab African countries, mainly to alleviate difficulties caused by the world economic crisis of 1973/74, which included increases in the price of oil.

In January 1974, in Cairo, the OAU Oil Committee and the ten countries of the Organization of Arab Petroleum-Exporting Countries (OAPEC) decided to establish the special Arab Aid Fund for Africa, with an initial capital of $200 million, to help African countries affected by the increases. The fund was set up within the secretariat of the Arab League as a temporary stop-gap arrangement, and it was to be transferred and amalgamated with BADEA when the latter became operational. The distribution of funds is effected by special arrangements between the OAU and the Arab League, and these arrangements are to remain in force until all existing funds are exhausted. Within two years the Special Fund had allocated $167.5 million to 31 different states. Table VII shows the distribution of this aid fund during 1974 and 1975.

3. Fund for Arab-African Technical Assistance (FAATA)

Created at around the same time as BADEA and SAFA, FAATA differs in that it deals with both Arab and African countries, and is particularly concerned with promoting economic and technical co-operation between them. It was approved in December 1973 by the Arab League with an initial capital of $15 million which was increased to $25 million at the Seventh Arab Summit.

Technical assistance can of course mean many things from providing skilled workers for a multi-million dollar feasibility study, to exchanging teachers at secondary or university level. At present the scope of this particular fund has been defined in only very general terms, but once this is narrowed down it is

TABLE VII

Loans from the Special Arab Fund for Africa

	State	Value of each instalment in US$	Date of signature for first instalment	Date of signature for second instalment
1	Botswana	2,700,000	1. 2.1975	27. 2.1975
2	Burundi	1,000,000	3.12.1974	29. 4.1975
3	Cameroon	2,850,000	To be paid by Af. Development Bank	19. 2.1975
4	Ivory Coast	3,600,000	——	——
5	Benin	1,200,000	17.12.1974	——
6	Ethiopia	7,100,000	25. 1.1975	1. 2.1975
7	Gambia	350,000	24.10.1974	11. 6.1975
8	Ghana	4,400,000	To be paid by the African Development Bank	27. 5.1975 9
9	Guinea	800,000	——	——
10	Guinea Bissau	250,000	2.12.1974	To be paid by the African Development Bank
11	Equatorial Guinea	250,000	10.11.1974	5. 2.1975
12	Upper Volta	2,700,000	To be paid by the African Development Bank	9. 2.1975
13	Mauritius	1,350,000	15. 2.1975	18. 3.1975
14	Kenya	1,800,000	23. 1.1975	11. 2.1975
15	Lesotho	1,400,000	16.12.1974	24. 5.1975
16	Liberia	1,800,000	17.10.1974	1. 4.1975
17	Madagascar	2,400,000	18.11.1974	11. 9.1975
18.	Malawi	3,750,000	14.11.1974	——
19	Mali	3,900,000	28.10.1974	14. 5.1975
20	Niger	2,700,000	To be paid by the African Development Bank	30. 1.1975
21	Uganda	5,650,000	13.10.1974	20. 1.1975
22	Rwanda	1,000,000	3.11.1974	11. 2.1975
23	Central African Empire	1,200,000	21.11.1974	29. 1.1975
24	Senegal	3,750,000	15. 1.1975	13. 3.1975
25	Sierra Leone	1,800,000	7.12.1974	12. 2.1975
26	Swaziland	2,100,000	27. 1.1975	25. 2.1975
27	Tanzania	7,100,000	17.10.1974	15. 2.1975
28	Chad	4,400,000	6.11.1974	1. 2.1975
29	Togo	900,000	To be paid by the African Development Bank	——
30	Zambia	6,350,000	28.12.1974	10. 3.1975
31	Zaire	6,200,000	8. 6.1975	8. 6.1975
32	Sao Tome & Principe	500,000	31. 8.1975	——

TOTAL LOANS TO THE AFRICAN COUNTRIES .... US $ 163,750,000
Paid to the Democratic Republic of Somalia ....US $ 7,500,000
Grand Total .... US $ 171,250,000

likely to overlap with other financial resources available to African countries. It will then be necessary for the Arab Secretariat to augment the resources of this Fund with monies from other Arab and African financial and technical assistance institutions. FAATA is still in an embryonic stage but there are good signs that it will soon be operative.

4. The Islamic Development Bank

The Islamic Development Bank was established in Jeddah in August 1974. As the name itself suggests it is a development bank designed to serve the interests of Islamic countries. Among its members are some African and other non-Arab Muslim countries. It has a subscribed capital of $2.4 billion.

5. Arab National Development Funds

These are also institutions for bilateral co-operation which are orientated partially or totally towards Africa. They include —

The Kuwait Fund: set up in 1961 with an initial capital of US$680 million, which has now been increased to US$3.4 billion. This Fund offers some of the most favourable terms in the world. The loans are on average spread over a period of 10 to 25 years, with an annual rate of interest of 3% to 4%.

The Abu Dhabi Fund: established in 1971 with an initial capital of US$126 million, which has now been increased to US$500 million. It was originally set up to cater for the interests of Arab countries, but of late it has made generous contributions to developments in African countries south of Sahara.

The Libyan Arab Foreign Bank: several African countries including Uganda have received financial assistance from Libya. Most of this aid has been channelled through the Libyan Arab Foreign Bank. The Bank has several branches in Africa.

The Saudi Development Fund: established in May 1974 with an initial capital of US$2.8 billion. A number of African countries have received technical and development aid from the Saudi Fund.

BADEA's VITAL ROLE

BADEA is probably the most important Arab financial instrument for channelling funds into African development projects. The decision to establish it was taken during the Sixth Arab Summit Conference, held in Algiers from 26 to 28 November 1973, soon after all member-States of the OAU had given unqualified support to the Arabs during the 1973 Arab-Israeli conflict. It has been said that the Arabs were repaying a debt of gratitude to the African countries who had broken off relations with Israel. But many Africans regard this as an insult to Africa, to African dignity and to African values. Their decision to sever relations with Israel was based on humanitarian principles alone. They were sympathetic to the Palestinians who had been made to flee their homeland.

Although the decision to establish the Bank was made in November 1973, it was not until January 1975, during the first Board of Governors' meeting in Cairo, that a formal agreement was signed.

Dr Ayari, Chairman of the Board of Directors and President of BADEA, who is himself a leading proponent of Afro-Arab co-operation, believes that when the Arab Heads of State established BADEA in July 1973 it was to express their collective political will to organize and strengthen co-operation with the African continent. There is however another school of thought which believes that BADEA was a response by the Arab League to the criticism from African leaders that Arab oil-producing countries were not providing special oil facilities for Africa, particularly the least developed countries.

Neither of these views provides an explanation for why the decision to set up the Bank was taken immediately after the Africans had given full support to the Arabs during the 1973 conflict with Israel. We believe that it was largely coincidental, and that OAU member-States supported the Arabs because of their dislike for colonialism in all its manifestations. Their support for the liberation of Arab-occupied territories was inspired by similar ideals to those that make the Arab countries support Africa over the liberation of Zimbabwe and Namibia and in the fight against apartheid in South Africa, That the decision to establish BADEA was taken in 1973 is simply because this was the year that OPEC increased the price of oil so that member-States found themselves with substantial financial surpluses. If the setting up of BADEA had a political objective it was to assert the Arab presence in Africa.

If the Bank is properly managed over the next five years it should accumulate enough information and expertise to make it an excellent mouthpiece for the views of either side. The Arab League charged the Bank with the responsibility of financing projects submitted by African Governments. They wanted it to be a new instrument of *bona fide* aid to development. They were convinced that its assets, coupled with flexible credit terms, would play an important role in the economic development of Africa. Its role is special in two aspects: first, it is the only major institution that exclusively promotes multilateral co-operation between Africa and the Arab world; and secondly, its capital comes exclusively from Arab countries and is only used to the benefit of non-Arab countries of Africa.

BADEA has its headquarters in Khartoum, Sudan. The University of Khartoum has a strong bias towards Afro-Arab studies, so BADEA is able to draw on useful experience when dealing with Afro-Arab issues. The Board of Governors, consisting of the Finance Ministers of the 18 member countries, is the supreme authority of the Bank. At its first meeting in Cairo on 11 January 1975, the Board of Governors elected Dr Ayari as President of the Bank and Chairman of the Board of Directors for a five-year renewable period. The Board of Directors consists of eleven members who are elected every four years, and they are entrusted with the management of the business of the Bank. Any member holding 200 shares or more has one seat on the Board of Directors.

The main features of BADEA's operation are as follows

1. BADEA's aid is designed to finance specific development projects, and as such cannot be used to replenish the Treasuries (recurrent expenditures) or improve the balances of payments of African countries. In the case of balance of payments deficits caused by increases in the prices of oil, oil-exporting countries have set up a special Fund to assist African countries who have been badly affected.

2. Planned projects, i.e. those which come within the framework of a national development plan, are considered favourably by the Bank. The Bank may reject a project which the government concerned considers to be of top priority if it is thought by the Bank that such a project would not contribute to the achievement of the objectives of the development plan of that country. For example, a huge expenditure on arms in Africa will not create more jobs, and yet employment is one of the goals of most African development plans. Generally, the Bank takes into consideration those projects that would help to achieve an economic and social equilibrium between the various regions and populations of the African countries concerned.
3. In the past some African countries have undertaken projects which bear no relation either to other projects or to the economic and social life of the nation. In order to do so they have taken on extremely expensive 'tied' loans which have been detrimental to their economies. In order to avoid such pitfalls, the Bank generally insists that projects which are financed by it should be put to international bidding between the suppliers of goods and services for the project.
4. With the agreement of recipient countries the Bank establishes procedures to follow up and keep a check on the projects which it finances. This is necessary since BADEA is accountable to its shareholders for the proper use of its funds to finance viable projects, and for the repayment of loans in accordance with the terms and conditions laid down by the Bank.
5. The credit terms of the Bank are flexible so that they can be adapted to specific features of a particular project with due regard to the economic and financial situation prevailing in the country concerned. By means of this diversification of credit terms, the Bank is able both to ensure maximum return for the utilization of its resources and to urge African countries, if need be, to reconsider some of their priorities.
6. The Bank may not take part in any operation whatsoever

that is contrary to, or likely to restrict or modify, its function.

7. The Bank may not undertake any operation in an African country if the country concerned objects to it.
8. The Bank shall take all necessary steps to ensure that the loans made are used for the purpose for which they were made available.
9. In its financing operations, the Bank shall take into consideration the ability of the recipient, or, as the case may be, of the recipient's guarantor to fulfil its obligations.
10. The Bank set out, right from the beginning, to co-ordinate its operations closely with those of other development institutions. It is hoped that BADEA will eventually serve as a centre for joint planning and co-ordination so as to harmonize the multilateral and bilateral aid of Arab countries to Africa.

It should be noted that when BADEA was first established many African governments questioned the appropriateness, and even the rationality, of creating a new institution that would play a similar role to the African Development Bank set up ten years earlier. The African Development Bank had high hopes and excellent objectives on paper but it has lamentably failed to achieve these because of lack of funds. Most of its allocations to African countries are of less than US$ 2 million, which is insufficient to make a meaningful impact on the untapped resources of Africa.

In response to African criticism, the senior executives of BADEA argued that the Bank was not simply an organization to recycle petro-dollars. It was neither a rival of ADB, nor a manoeuvre to impose Arab influence in Africa. It was and still is an institution for co-operation with Africa, and its aim is to participate as an equal partner with African states in the economic development of Africa. The results of the Bank's operations so far have demonstrated that it is a genuinely international financial institution which is keen to understand the development needs of Africa and co-ordinate financial aid on the African continent.

In order to achieve its overall objective of co-operation for development, BADEA has set up links with international and other development institutions such as ADB, IBRD, EDF and UN Specialized Agencies, especially UNDP, FAO and UNIDO. Co-operation with other institutions with similar objectives was seen to be particularly important for two reasons:

— so that BADEA might benefit from the experience and expertise accumulated by these institutions in Africa;
— so that concerted action might be taken with these institutions, within the scope permitted by the policies of BADEA, to finance Africa's development.

In certain cases formal agreements have been signed. In May 1975 BADEA's President Dr Chedly Ayari, and Mr Abdelwaheb Labid on behalf of the ADB-ADF, signed an agreement which provided for the following:

1. exchange of information relating to studies carried out on various aspects of economic development in Africa;
2. periodic top-level meetings following a schedule to be outlined;
3. organization of joint undertakings with a view to identifying the development needs of Africa;
4. collaboration between BADEA and the ADB-ADF in the field of staff training;
5. joint financing of development projects that are of value to Africa.

On 17 April 1975 similar arrangements were made between Dr Ayari and Mr Robert McNamara, the President of the International Bank for Reconstruction and Development. Mr McNamara said that the World Bank's main concern was to see that sources of finance were transferred to the developing countries for economic development. For this reason, the World Bank welcomed close co-operation with BADEA, and was prepared to make available its list of projects under consideration in Africa.

ADVANTAGES OF BADEA LOANS

The terms and conditions of the loans issued by BADEA are concessionary: interest rates range from one to six per cent. The discrimination in the interest charged depends on several factors such as the nature of the project — commercial or noncommercial — and the state of the economy of the borrower. The repayment period is staggered over 25 years, normally with a five year grace period before the repayment begins.

Article 4 of the Charter of the Bank provides for the parties that may take advantage of the Bank's operations. These include:

— the governments of African countries that are not members of the League of Arab States,
— public and private financial and development institutions in the African countries referred to above,
— joint Arab-African financial and development institutions,
— any other financial and development organizations and institutions carrying out economic projects in Africa.

Thus, although all the aid given by the Bank up to now has been made exclusively to African governments and development institutions, it is possible for private companies to qualify.

FINANCIAL RESOURCES OF BADEA

The capital stock of the Bank, as initially subscribed, is US$231 million. This may be increased by the subscriptions of new members or by the additional subscription of an existing member. The Charter also states that the Bank should endeavour to increase its resources by borrowing, by obtaining sureties and long and medium term markets — at such times as it can start this type of transaction without jeopardizing either its solvency or its purpose and function with regard to development financing. At the time of writing the Bank has not resorted to borrowing.

The States listed here (Table VIII) are the original members of the Bank. Any Arab State is entitled to become a party to the agreement establishing the Bank.

BADEA'S STRATEGY DURING 1976-1980

Since BADEA, however ambitious, is a young financial institution its future activities can for the time being only be viewed in a medium-term perspective, that is, up to 1980. For the period under consideration the Bank has ambitious programmes which will necessitate an increase in its financial

TABLE VIII

Subscriptions of members to the capital stock of the Arab Bank for the Economic Development in Africa

Country	Amount (in US $)
The Hashemite Kingdom of Jordan	1,000,000
The United Arab Emirates	20,000,000
The State of Bahrain	1,000,000
The Tunisian Republic	5,000,000
The Democratic and Popular Republic of Algeria	20,000,000
The Kingdom of Saudi Arabia	50,000,000
The Democratic Republic of Sudan	1,000,000
The Syrian Arab Republic	1,000,000
The Republic of Iraq	30,000,000
The Sultanate of Oman	4,000,000
The State of Qatar	20,000,000
The State of Kuwait	20,000,000
The Lebanese Republic	5,000,000
The Libyan Arab Republic	40,000,000
The Arab Republic of Egypt	1,000,000
The Kingdom of Morocco	10,000,000
The Islamic Republic of Mauritania	1,000,000
Palestine	1,000,000
TOTAL:	231,000,000

resources.

At the time of writing BADEA was committed to finance projects in 20 African countries. In its five year programme its financial involvement between 1975 and 1980 was set out as shown here (Table IX).

It would appear, therefore, that for the period 1975 to 1980 BADEA's global financial involvement would amount to US$1.235 billion, which is about US$200 million per year. Since the population of Africa is roughly about 250 million, the average distribution of this aid per capita would remain

TABLE IX
(in million US $)

1975	1976	1977	1978	1979	1980
85.5	120.00	250.00	250.00	250.00	250.00

slightly below one dollar. This is a very appreciable contribution considering that the donors are themselves developing countries who need money for their own economic development.

According to studies carried out by BADEA, African investment requirements will amount to about US$4 billion annually. This is three times the amount Africa is getting now. The Bank has estimated the supplementary global aid from Arab countries between 1976 and 1980 at US$1 billion per year, an estimate which does not take into account petrol aid. These figures give some idea of the size of the problem and the amount of capital that Arab-Africa co-operation will involve during the next five years.

BADEA's ambitious programme cannot be achieved unless there is sufficient capital available. After taking into account the number of countries eligible for financial assistance (40 countries), and the number of viable projects in the pipeline, there could be no doubt that the initial capital of US$231 million was inadequate. The Board of Governors of BADEA therefore agreed to increase it to US$1 billion, the increase to be affected as follows:

1. a first increase of BADEA's capital by US$269 million, which will raise subscribed capital to US$500 million starting from 1 January 1977;
2. a second increase by US$500 million, which will raise BADEA's subscribed capital to US$1 billion between 1 January 1978 and 1 January 1980.

This scheme of increasing the Bank's capital conforms both to the provisions of the Charter and to the Bank's operational programme for the period 1976-1980.

TYPES OF PROJECTS FOR BADEA

BADEA does not impose projects or programmes on African

States. It will give priority to projects in the following sectors:
— farming and agriculture, food industries;
— exploitation of natural resources;
— infrastructure;
— industries that include an adequate percentage of African 'value added';
— training of African personnel;
— development-related services such as transport and tourism.

Except for special cases the Bank's contribution to any particular project in any given country shall not exceed US$10 million and without exception the Bank shall be involved in the follow-up of project implementation. This is in accordance with the terms, conditions and procedures which are agreed upon by the parties concerned when such an agreement is drawn up. Recipient countries do not normally object to this provision because they regard BADEA as a genuine and dependable partner in the economic development of Africa. As a rule, foreign financial and technical assistance is there to supplement the efforts of nationals of the countries concerned; so the Bank's participation in any financial operation is often matched by a reasonable contribution from the recipient.

The currency used in the Bank's operation is the United States dollar, but the recipient may draw the loan in any other currency subject to prior authorization by the Bank. Generally speaking, the Bank does not pay for local costs but rather provides assistance for procurement abroad. However, in exceptional cases, such as the construction of 40 kilometres road between Kitwe and Ndola, a project involving very little foreign cost, the recipient African country or firm may be allowed to draw part or the whole of the loan in local currency, subject to the conditions set forth in the loan. The Bank does not part with its money until the African governments or their authorized representatives, such as Central Banks, provide the necessary guarantees. Guarantee requirements are an integral part of the loan agreement, and the Bank ensures that no disbursement may be made on a loan until such time as the guarantee agreement becomes effective.

In order to stimulate employment in Africa and the Arab World, Arab and African bidders are often given preferential treatment in the case of international tenders, provided that the difference in cost does not exceed 10 per cent. Goods and services which include a certain percentage of Arab, African or mixed 'value added' shall be deemed to be of Arab, African or mixed Arab-African origin, the percentage required being set by the Bank on the basis of the case submitted to it. As regards the procurement of goods and services, other things being equal, the Bank advocates the principle of international tenders in order to obtain competitive offers. Companies which are boycotted by Arab States for carrying on business with Israel are excluded from tendering in the projects financed by the Bank.

BADEA and the ADB

A few additional comments need to be made on the relations between BADEA and the ADB. When BADEA was established under the direction of the Arab League it was received with mixed feelings in various African capitals. There was one school of thought which believed that the African response to the setting up of the Bank should be to restrict membership of the ADB to non-Arab African States. In March 1977 at the Cairo Summit, some of the African leaders argued that any Bank on the African continent belongs to Africans and to African Arabs. According to them BADEA is an Arab Bank for Africa whose orientation and policy are set by the Arab countries (some of which are also African). They concluded from this that BADEA was a party to the planned co-operation of Arab and African countries, and that it should therefore be Africanized to enable it to play its role on an equal footing with the ADB in developing this co-operation. In their opinion it was desirable for African States to become members of BADEA to make sure the Bank did not become like the EIB (European Investment Bank) which also contributes to Africa's development.

These arguments show that there has been some uncertainty over the function and status of BADEA. BADEA is unlike the ADB in that it is not the financial organ of a political institution. If we take the World Bank group of financial institutions, these are clearly related to the United Nations. At the African level the ADB is the financial organ of the OAU; at the Arab League level, however, the financial arm is AFESD and not BADEA. BADEA is thus in a special category.

Now that BADEA has been operational for more than two years, the difference between it and other African and Arab financial institutions is becoming clearer. BADEA serves to direct Arab funds into African countries to finance development projects and to provide technical assistance. The ADB exists primarily to promote economic co-operation amongst the member-States of the OAU. Both BADEA and the ADB thus have well-defined but separate strategies and programmes of action. The ADB uses funds subscribed by member-States of the OAU and sometimes borrows from the international capital markets of the world or from other international financial institutions. BADEA handles only Arab funds and is becoming the major financial institution for Afro-Arab economic co-operation.

Now that some of the initial problems have been settled the two Banks have agreed to meet regularly to compare notes and at times formulate common policies and objectives and agree on common guidelines for action. The first meeting of BADEA and ADB took place in March 1975, in Dakar. The meeting was primarily an Annual Meeting of the African Development Bank and the African Development Fund. BADEA was formally invited to attend and participate in the discussions without the right to vote.

The joint meeting of BADEA and ADB discussed specifically the drawing up of medium- and long-term strategies for Arab-African co-operation. The strategies were to be based on the setting up of specific programmes of action and effective institutions of co-operation. It was agreed that the absence of proper co-ordination between existing funds had resulted either in duplication of work or fruitless efforts, and it was therefore decided that institutional collaboration must take place at various levels, i.e. at the level of the Arab League, the OAU, the ADB, the ECA and BADEA.

Contrary to the expectations of the prophets of doom, the meeting of the ADB and BADEA in Dakar opened up new avenues for co-operation between the two Banks. Soon after the Dakar Conference the Annual Meeting of the ADB and the ADF was held in Kinshasa, from 3-8 May 1975. At this meeting Dr Ayari pursued the theme of Afro-Arab co-operation, and he particularly stressed the importance of co-operation between the ADB and BADEA and of defining a concerted financial strategy. Alongside these annual meetings, a meeting of the heads of African regional and sub-regional development banks also took place at which BADEA was represented. The participants at the meeting agreed both as individual development banks and collectively as regional or sub-regional banks to co-operate with BADEA in fulfilling the task of economic development.

The ADB and BADEA have agreed to co-operate on preliminary project studies and in the checking and monitoring of projects financed by the two institutions. They have also agreed that it is possible to go further and to arrive at a real division of labour, enabling better utilization of the human resources and expertise at their disposal.

Financial co-operation between the ADB, the ADF and BADEA means, in real terms, placing at the disposal of Africa three complementary sources of long-term loans at very low interest rates: this would amount to no less than US$1,000 million (ADB $500 million, ADF $300 million, and BADEA $230 million). All three institutions have plans to increase their capital base, and if their plans come to fruition the available funds to Africa by 1980 would be of the order of US$2,400 million or an average of $500 million a year. At Kinshasa, Dr Ayari proposed that a joint ADB-BADEA Commission be made responsible for the common financial strategy.

The Secretary-General of the Arab League has stated that his organization has entrusted to BADEA management of the Arab Special Fund for Aid to Africa, which has already distributed nearly US$170 million to non-Arab African farmers. BADEA intends to review, in close collaboration with the ADB, the criteria for use of these funds which are intended for emergency aid or assistance with oil purchases. This is in line with the agreement to compare notes on all aspects of economic development in Africa. It is also in line with the decision made at Kinshasa by the ADB and BADEA to do everything possible to:

1. set up a joint BADEA-ADB Committee for the implementation of the recommendations of the Dakar Arab-African Ministers' Conference;
2. set up, with the OAU and the Arab League, a special committee to rethink and reorganize the methods and criteria for allocation of the resources of the Arab Special Fund for Aid to Africa (this is in response to one of the decisions of the Dakar Conference);
3. undertake systematic co-ordination of their efforts by organizing meetings several times a year between the operating departments of the two institutions.

In addition to the ADB and ADF, BADEA is co-operating with all regional and sub-regional development banks. Some of the African development banks have agreed with BADEA to increase co-operation. Already several sectors have been identified as areas in which joint action could be taken. These include:

1. methods of co-financing;
2. collaboration aimed at the mobilization of financial and human resources;
3. exchange of information about projects and programmes;
4. conducting of joint studies;
5. agreements as to working methods, the definitions and preparations of projects, etc. (in order to carry out this policy, regular meetings are planned: the first took place at the technical level and was held at Abidjan on 15 June 1975).

BADEA can be said to act as a central agency for Arab financial institutions which want to help Africa. It has established a good working relation with the majority of Arab financial institutions such as the Kuwait Fund, the Abu Dhabi Fund, the Saudi Fund, the Iraq Fund, the Islamic Development Bank, and so on. Periodic meetings are planned to enable senior executives of all these institutions to examine aspects of present and future Arab policy for financing economic developments projects in Africa.

By the end of this decade the dream of Dr Ayari could become a reality: when BADEA was established he stated that

Arab-African co-operation must be co-ordinated and institutionalized. He believed that without co-ordination Arab-African co-operation would be unable to play any significant role in Africa's development. He pressed for good institutions, efficient machinery and co-ordinated effort. The co-operation between the ADB and BADEA, and the good relationship between BADEA and other Arab financial institutions geared to participate in the economic development of Africa, can be seen as the beginnings of institutionalized co-ordinated co-operation.

CHAPTER SIX

ARAB INVESTMENT IN AFRICA

The experts who participated in the Afro-Arab Symposium held in December 1976 in Sharjah, one of the United Arab Emirates, recognized the important role played by international capital and investment in the economic development of, and transfer of resources and technology to, the developing world. They accordingly resolved that the conditions that govern or influence international capital movements, and in particular the transfer of financial resources to the developing countries, can and must be improved. They observed that the economic development which has taken place in the United Arab Emirates within the past five years has been due to the timely arrival of the 'Arab Dollar' which has been accompanied by technical know-how from the industrialized countries. Similar development has, of course, taken place in all Arab countries where oil has produced Arab dollars in abundance.

There was a general consensus among the participants at the symposium that there is a close relationship between continuity of investment flows and the stability of the terms on which such flows are admitted. It was however emphasized that capital outflow to Africa should be consistent with the national objectives of the recipient countries. Only in this way can such investments make an optimum contribution to the fulfilment of African economic development plans.

The success of Afro-Arab economic co-operation will depend upon the following factors:

1. Political decisions must be taken by Arab countries to invest in African enterprises.
2. The Afro-Arab countries concerned should take appropriate steps to ensure that private investment is carried out in harmony with the development policies and objectives of the recipient country.
3. Capital likes to go where it is safe and is likely to yield a high return. The host government should therefore improve the security of investment.
4. A climate of mutual confidence is indispensable for

increasing the volume of direct investment.

5. The recipient country should give a clear indication of the policy under which it wishes to obtain external private investment.
6. Arab countries should, to the extent that their constitutions permit, facilitate non-discriminatory access of African countries to the various Arab Funds.
7. Arab countries should provide information regarding access to their Funds, and also clarify the regulations and practices of Arab financial institutions.
8. African countries should inform prospective Arab investors of their economic situations and policies.
9. Measures to increase capital flows to African countries should be taken jointly by the OAU and the Arab League.
10. Efforts should also be made at international levels to promote or facilitate international investment. Such efforts could include bilateral and multilateral collaboration.

Whilst it is not possible to generalize about the nature of investment climate, since conditions both in the Arab world and in Africa differ from country to country, it is nevertheless clear that foreign investment can make a substantial contribution to development. Investment can result in the transfer of technological, managerial and other associated skills as well as increasing output and employment and strengthening the balance of payments. However, recipient countries should seek to retain overall control, and investors should *expect* to use local labour.

The recipient country should give investment incentives such as tax holidays, generous tax allowances and reasonable tax rates. Capital-exporting countries should give reciprocal incentives to those of their nationals who want to invest in developing countries. The Afro-Arab situation is complicated by the fact that Arab countries are themselves in the process of development, and as such they often offer similar or better investment incentives than African ones: the United Arab Emirates, for example, have no direct tax, and indirect tax on luxury imports does not exceed 3%.

It must be recognized too that some African countries, particularly those engaged in mining, need more money than they can get either through aid or private investment. This means that they have to go to the capital market to borrow the huge sums of money required for their development expenditure. The same is true for some Arab oil-producing countries who have deficits in their balance of payments.

Developing countries, however, are generally discriminated against in the capital markets of industrialized countries. What Afro-Arab countries should do together with other affected nations of the Third World is to ask the developed countries concerned to relax credit restrictions and take steps to remove obstacles hindering the access of developing countries to the capital markets. These measures should cover:

A. *Conditions governing the granting of bank loans to non-residents*

1. The removal of quantative restrictions on the provision of financing to non-residents;
2. the relaxing of the rules governing the currency denomination of loans to non-residents;
3. the elimination of interest rate differentials between loans to residents and non-residents of similar credit-worthiness.

B. *Rules governing foreign securities and portfolios held by non-Bank financial institutions*

Elimination of rules providing for differential treatment based on the borrowing country and on the status of the borrower.

C. *Euro Markets*

1. Relaxation of restrictions regarding the currencies used by developing country borrowers in loans and bonds issued;
2. simplification of the prospectuses that have to be presented to enable operations to be registered;
3. relaxation of deposit requirements for developing countries;
4. relaxation of restrictions placed on the public offer of securities to prospective investors;
5. authorities of developed countries should take a liberal view of bonds denominated in their own currency, issued by developing countries.

The above comments suggest that if private capital markets, which are funded in part by Arab dollars, are to provide sufficient sums to developing countries on reasonable terms, then they will have to become more flexible. This will involve policy action at the official level, both national and international. What is needed are incentives designed to stimulate the flow of private capital both to African countries and to those Arab countries not endowed with oil. These incentives should be in the form of favourable fiscal treatment of income derived from loans to economically disadvantaged countries. Credits to such countries should be exempted from ceilings on domestic credit expansion.

The Arab oil-exporting countries could use their newly-acquired strength to influence international organizations such as the IBRD and the IMF to open their doors more to those countries which are both economically and geographically disadvantaged. In particular, they should ask the international organizations to undertake measures in the following areas:

1. The principle of co-financing is supported by members of the IBRD and IMF; but the developing countries feel that it should be improved and expanded. Co-financing should not result in a reduction in the lending programme of the international financial organizations, either overall or for any individual country. Co-financing to countries like Zambia and Algeria, with ready access to the capital markets, should not affect the total volume of funds which they are entitled to borrow. The principal characteristic of co-financing should therefore be its additionality.
2. There is a general consensus among those developing countries who are members of IMF and IBRD that international organizations should examine the possibility of placing part of their portfolio with institutional investors, which have not up to now been operating together with the developing countries: the lending capacity of these international organizations would be increased and new sources of financing made available to the developing countries.
3. In various international forums including UNCTAD,

IBRD and IMF, developing countries have collectively appealed for the reserves of international financial institutions to be invested in the developing countries. The international reserve position and prospects of the countries concerned would naturally be taken into account in order to safeguard the investment.

TECHNICAL ASSISTANCE

Prospective investors, both private and public, have on occasion rejected projects where no proper feasibility studies accompanied the proposals. A number of Arab officials, for example, (in particular from Kuwait and Saudi Arabia) have defended their governments' inability to lend money to African countries on precisely these grounds. They say that African countries wishing to apply for loans must submit feasibility studies explaining not only the finances of the projects but also their place in the overall development of the countries' economies.

To overcome this problem, international organizations such as IBRD should provide additional technical assistance to the developing nations. Undertaking the kind of feasibility studies for which the Arab financial experts are asking requires money. Such studies are often expensive and if they prove that the project is not a viable one, the money spent on them could be construed as having been wasted. It is therefore recommended that feasibility studies, wherever possible, should be undertaken either by the country in which the development will take place or by those international financial organizations and institutions in a position to do so. Here it should be recorded with appreciation that the EEC has agreed to undertake feasibility studies for the African, Caribbean and Pacific States associated with the Community under the EEC-ACP Convention of Lomé. This will apply both to projects which they themselves will finance and to projects which are to be financed by other donors or investors. It is hoped that other industrialised countries will adopt the same approach.

The Arab League and the OAU should also direct their competent institutions to prepare financial survey and pre-investment studies, and should set up training and research organizations in which young Afro-Arab men and women may learn modern technology. These organizations should be specifically adapted to the needs of Arab and African countries.

PROBLEMS

The subject of private investment in Africa is a sensitive one since in the minds of both Arabs and Africans it is associated with colonialism and exploitation. This unease is justified to the extent that much of the current foreign investment in developing countries brings little benefit to the host country. What we shall be discussing in this section is the extent to which, with proper safeguards, the situation could be improved.

The first point which is crucial is that the sovereignty of the host country must always remain intact. Under no circumstances must the host government lose the right to govern. No foreign investor should be able to dictate the conditions under which he is going to carry on business. He should be encouraged to accommodate his business interests in the overall economic policies of the host country.

Recent studies on the operations of multinational corporations have acted as an eye-opener for some developing countries. The most serious issue centres around the extent to which foreign investment causes the economy of a country to be controlled from outside. This has raised the question of whether the income accruing to foreigners as a result of investment is justified in relation to the benefits accruing to the host country. It has been suggested that the best approach by a host country is to determine the impact of each foreign investment operation on its national objectives, in order to see what effect such an investment will have on employment, foreign exchange, tax revenues, self-reliance, etc. If the investment under review passes the test, the final consideration should be to define the cheapest method of maximizing these benefits.

The term 'foreign investment' is a misnomer when it refers to businesses using local funds. It is not unusual in Africa to find firms and businesses owned by people of Asian origin and wholly financed by local banks describing themselves as foreign investors simply because the owners are not nationals. In such cases the benefits of foreign exchange are lost if local funds are used. Such businesses should only be allowed to remain in foreign hands if they provide a service to the community which cannot be fulfilled under local management.

Foreign investment is not often directed towards infrastructural projects. Private investors prefer commercial projects which are likely to yield good returns within the shortest possible period. If foreign capital were to be invested in export-oriented industries this would contribute to the foreign exchange requirements of the host country and as such it should be encouraged. At present, however, most of the capital flow goes to the primary commodity sector whose products are subject to considerable price instability on world markets. Much more benefit would accrue if private investment were channelled into manufacturing industries, whose products are increasing in value on the international market.

One of the drawbacks of foreign investment is that it almost always involves the recipient country in the expense of patents, licences and other software; this is often the only way for a developing country to obtain technological and management assistance. However, although it is costly to lease patents, foreign investment does at least make them available to those developing countries which cannot afford to buy them. Taxation is of interest both to foreign investors and to host countries, and it is an area in which there appears to be a good deal of uncertainty and misunderstanding. During UNCTAD IV as well as at the North-South Dialogue in Paris industrialized countries argued that if developing countries wanted to attract foreign investment they should offer more attractive concessions, especially as regards tax allowances and tax holidays. Most African countries have brought in investment laws offering foreign capital and enterprise a wide range of incentives including accelerated depreciation concessions, partial or complete exemption from tax and custom duties, guarantees of profits and capital repatriation — all these being offered at the expense of government revenue or the balance of payments. The response has been, to say the least, very disappointing, and private investors sometimes try to deprive the host country of even its legal revenue by either tax avoidance or tax evasion. This is often achieved through the internal pricing policies of a parent company. The subsidiary company may buy imports from the parent company at inflated prices and thereby reduce its profits.

Mining contracts deserve special mention here because of the problems they have caused to some African countries. Most of these agreements were concluded on, or prior to, independence when most laws in Africa and Arab countries favoured colonial investors. The agreements were often drawn up entirely in favour of the investor. Any subsequent attempt by the host countries to renegotiate the agreements have generated charges of breach of faith and unfair treatment. Because of this, African and Arab countries now think twice before concluding similar agreements which may involve them in sensitive political dealings with the home countries of the investors. To avoid such disputes, any new contracts should be flexible: they should provide for periodic revisions, or include sliding scale arrangements whereby benefits to the government should increase if the operations turn out to be profitable. The cardinal rule should be an acceptance in good faith to renegotiate the agreements should a particular situation warrant it. What is important is for the foreign investor to appreciate the sovereign right of any state to reorganize its economy in the interests of the country as a whole.

With these general comments in mind, let us now look more closely at some of the considerations which influence private and institutional investors.

INVESTMENT CLIMATE

Foreign investors naturally want to know something about the investment climate of the countries in which they decide to invest, but in the current world economic situation there is already little stability. There is a certain irony in the demand by industrialized countries — who with all their resources and technological know-how have themselves failed to achieve stable economies — that developing countries should establish stable economic conditions in order to attract foreign capital.

Developing countries are often victims of circumstances beyond their control. Planning is done in a vacuum since they have no control over the price of their own raw materials. They operate in a buyer's market. Even during the boom period of the early sixties, when the economies of the industrialized world had recovered from the adverse effects of the Second World War, most developing countries registered negative growth. The industrialized world is well aware of the various and complex difficulties which continue to confront the developing nations, difficulties which have prevented their governments from ensuring even a basic standard of living for their people.

Developing countries know that it is in their own interest to have stability in order to plan their economic future. But is this possible? Up to three years ago foreign entrepreneurs considered Zambia a paradise: even those who brought nothing in with them could, if they managed to set up a simple business such as hair-dressing, benefit from generous exchange control regulations which allowed them to remit most their profits regardless of the nature of their business. This was so because copper, which is the mainstay of the economy, was earning a fair return on the international market. Suddenly the price was reduced from £1,200 per ton to £550 per ton. The new price constituted a negative return on investment and the Government was obliged to subsidize the industry in order to avoid massive social problems. Under such conditions the liberal foreign exchange regulations had to give way to more stringent ones in order to meet the new situation. New regulations needed to be brought in to deal with the problems arising from the absence of foreign exchange earnings. Developing countries therefore must take measures to protect themselves from the effects of large fluctuations in the prices of raw materials on the world market.

It is in the interest of both the investor and the host country to have a formal investment code as well as fiscal laws. In every developing country there are written fiscal laws but some of them do not have investment codes as such. In most cases the existing tax laws, exchange control regulations and other related rules would constitute the required code.

One of the problems with the establishment of investment codes is that many of the developing countries have been colonies until fairly recently and have not yet been able to reorganise their economies on a non-colonial basis. We can take the example of those countries which were under Portuguese rule: during the whole colonial period they had no budgets of their own. Everything was controlled, planned and co-ordinated from Portugal. It is scarcely surprising that at independence these countries should have been left without any foundation on which to establish fiscal laws and regulations.

Problems of this kind will take time to resolve. What a developing country willing to accept foreign investment should aim to establish is a clear political, economic and legal framework within which investment activities can be carried out. This would create a favourable climate for the flow of both official and private capital from outside. There must be a clear-cut programme of economic aims and priorities which would provide foreign investors with a reliable guide to the framework within which their commercial activities are feasible. In this way foreign investment would become more attractive.

TIMELY AND UNRESTRICTED TRANSFERS

Two questions of particular concern to the prospective investor in a country are whether the country allows unrestricted transfer of investment income, and whether capital can be easily repatriated at the end of the investment period.

Consider the cases of Zaire and the United Arab Emirates: the basic difference between the two as regards transfer of investment income is that the United Arab Emirates have sufficient foreign exchange earnings to fulfil all their foreign financial obligations, which means that they can allow prompt and unrestricted transfer of income accruing to foreign investors. Zaire on the other hand cannot afford to have a liberal foreign exchange policy. The difference arises from the fact that the major foreign exchange earner from Zaire is copper, whose current price on the world market is just high enough for the industry to break-even, while the economy of the United Arab Emirates is based on oil which is currently in great demand.

Timely and unrestricted transfer of income from investment, and repatriation of capital on the termination of the investment, can only be guaranteed by countries with adequate foreign exchange reserves. In the case of countries with balance of payments problems, the principle should be stated in the investment code with the following qualification: *subject to the availability of foreign reserves* the host country undertakes to permit transfer of income from investment, and *upon justifiable reasons* allow the repatriation of capital upon the termination of the investment. It is perhaps worth noting here that most of the industrialized countries could not at the moment afford to comply strictly with the principle of timely and unrestricted transfer of income if it were a condition imposed upon them by the IMF.

In cases where an investor decides of his own free will to terminate his investment, it is his responsibility to make appropriate arrangements. He can decide to sell his business either to nationals of the host country or to other foreign investors who may be interested. If the business is bought by nationals or foreign investors who are also carrying on business in the same country the payment will often be made in the local currency. In that event the normal foreign exchange regulations which are in force would apply. If the business is bought by foreign investors, then the buyer and the seller should come to an agreement on currency in accordance with the foreign exchange regulations of the host country. If the investor decides to liquidate his business he cannot expect to be granted timely and unrestricted repatriation of his capital. Normally an investor decides to liquidate his investment for speculative reasons, beneficial to him. In such a case he cannot expect the host government to relax its regulations.

NATIONALIZATION

It is not uncommon for investors to bring up the question of fair treatment in the event of their businesses being nationalized.

Invariably they demand prompt, adequate and effective compensation. The investor often gives a wider definition of nationalization than is generally accepted. For example it is argued that there are many actions which a host country can take which have similar effects to those of nationalization. These include excessive interference in management, forced sale of assets, confiscatory taxation and forced renegotiation of contracts.

Nationalization generally takes place only as a last resort. It is usually an attempt to make an industry more responsive to the needs of the country by providing more employment or producing more goods and services for the community. In the circumstances, it is reasonable for governments to compensate the owners.

Although there is no difficulty in accepting the principle of fair treatment in the event of nationalization there are often insurmountable problems associated with prompt and adequate compensation. Governments can only make prompt payment if foreign exchange reserves are sufficient to enable them to do so. A further problem is that it is often not clear what is meant by adequate compensation. One way of dealing with this problem is to reach a compromise price based on a comparison between the cost price and the market price of the business. Successful negotiation of compensation generally depends to a large extent on the amount of goodwill on either side.

In May 1976, during UNCTAD IV in Nairobi, the industrialized countries argued that the nationalization policy of a host country is an important part of a potential investor's view of the investment possibilities in that country. They contended that, under international law, investors have the right to expect that the taking of private property for public purpose will be non-discriminatory. The countries of the Third World, who for the purpose of the conference were referred to as the Group of 77, had no difficulty in accepting and appreciating the concern of Western investors. The Group of 77 stated that, in general, nationalization would only occur for a public purpose, and would be non-discriminatory; but they were not prepared to give assurances of prompt, adequate and effective compensation in the event. The industrialized countries had demanded such assurances as pre-requisites for private Western investment in the countries of the Third World. The Group of 77 argued that it is the right of each state to exercise full sovereignty over its national economic activities. It was further maintained that it is outside the scope of an international organization to set guidelines which may encroach upon the sovereignty of its member-states. It was suggested that the best possible course of action was for bilateral agreements to be entered into by the countries concerned. Such agreements could then contain reciprocal assurances.

IMPARTIAL ARBITRATION

Even with the best of intentions on all sides, investment disputes can arise. In cases where bilateral efforts are not successful in resolving investor/host country disagreement, investors sometimes suggest that governments should take advantage of the industrial arbitration facility provided by the World Bank's International Centre for the Settlement of Industrial Disputes.

Most developing countries do not subscribe to the idea of having recourse to the ICSID. They argue that disputes arising in a given state should be settled by the competent courts of that state. In some cases their constitutions specifically allow for investment disputes arising within their territorial boundaries to be settled by their courts. This is probably one of the reasons why more than half of the World Bank members are not members of ICSID.

Some industrialized countries, notably the USA and the Federal Republic of Germany, have special insurance schemes which facilitate the flow of private investment by insuring investors against certain risks. Economists have suggested establishing multilateral investment schemes which would provide assurances to investors in the countries of the Third World. It is widely believed that many opportunities for productive investment in developing countries are not exploited because of actual or potential political risks. This has resulted in an inefficient allocation of global financial resources and has impeded economic development in the

Third World.

These are some of the general problem areas relating to foreign investment. How does this relate to the question of Afro-Arab economic co-operation? In this context the term 'Arabs' refers to the Arab League and not the Arab countries either separately or in groups. A similar working definition is also essential for Africa. In the case of 'Africa' what is meant is the Organization of African Unity, not the African States individually or in groups. This is important since as we have stated before, African States are heterogeneous but the Organization of African Unity is a homogeneous organization bound by common aims and objectives which are clearly stated in its charter. One thing which is evident is the need for clearly defined policies and well-thought-out strategies for their implementation. This makes these two organisations, the Arab League and the OAU, crucial to the establishment of effective Afro-Arab economic co-operation.

The two Charters in their present form are inadequate to deal with the complex problems of modern economic development. When the oil crisis arose there was no mechanism for passing information to the OAU to alert them in advance. What happened was that information was exchanged through the international press. The local papers gathered what they called public opinion and presented it as reaction to the oil-price increases by OPEC countries. These reports finally found their way into the international papers and this naturally had a damaging effect on Afro-Arab relations. The Organization of African Unity on the other hand dealt with the explosive situation of the oil crisis of 1974 in an extremely diplomatic way. All its statements were of a conciliatory nature.

One of the problems raised at the Sharjah Symposium in December 1976 was that of the wording of documents. Translation is notoriously difficult and texts may have different implications in different languages; but the problem is not insurmountable. What is important is that there should be regular meetings between the OAU and the Arab League in order to avoid a repetition of the sort of situation that arose at the time of the oil crisis. If these two organizations are modified and strengthened to become the major organs of Afro-Arab economic co-operation, then it should be possible for them to work out clear and mutually acceptable investment policies and development strategies.

It is often necessary to set targets and periods within which given aims and objectives can be realized. We therefore propose that the initial phase of Afro-Arab co-operation should start with the Afro-Arab Summit Meeting in 1977 and end in December 1982. The advantage of choosing this period is that it will end before the Summit meeting of the OAU in 1983, which will review the work done during its second decade. The second decade of the OAU is expected to record tremendous improvements in the economic and political development of its members.

One final point to note is that Afro-Arab co-operation cannot be separated from African and Arab political and financial relations with other parts of the world. Indeed the economic crisis of 1973-75 has demonstrated beyond any reasonable doubt the importance of economic interdependence. The recent problems which have afflicted the international economy have underlined the need for the countries of the world to work together. In the interests of a well-organised economic order it may be necessary to adopt measures which may seem unpalatable to developed countries.

In order to achieve the new international economic order the international community should endeavour to make substantial progress in such areas as trade, transfer of capital resources, debt adjustments, monetary reforms, the transfer and development of appropriate technology to and within developing countries, etc. International organizations have vital role to play. They should:

— improve the effective participation of developing countries in the policy- and decision-making processes at all levels within these institutions by increasing their voting power. (OPEC countries are now some of the major donors to various schemes of the International Monetary Fund and the World Bank: they should be accorded corresponding voting powers);
— make their policies more responsive to development needs,

particularly by adapting the terms and conditions, and the real volume, of their assistance to the Third World.

The international financial institutions should make appropriate changes in their operational and financial policies within the framework of their statutory provisions in order to:

— establish pre-investment funds for the preparation of joint projects in developing countries (this is provided for under the Lomé Convention);
— provide resources for giving loans for joint projects in developing countries;
— provide a part of their resources for the equity financing of joint enterprises established by developing countries;
— stimulate, by giving financial support, the establishment of associations of primary product producers in the developing countries;
— stimulate, by giving financial support, the establishment of joint enterprises in developing countries for the marketing and transport of goods and commodities;
— provide financing for joint development schemes and projects in developing countries;
— establish new, and expand the existing, export credit finance and export credit insurance schemes for increasing trade among developing countries;
— contribute to the establishment and development of regional financial markets in developing countries.

In order to establish and implement the measures outlined above, international organizations will have to work in concert with regional Development Banks in Africa and the Arab world.

As part of their contribution to the new international economic order the developed countries could contribute to the expansion and intensification of co-operation among developing countries, thereby improving conditions for co-operation between developing and developed countries. The developed countries should:

— demonstrate their political willingness to support the efforts of co-operation among developing countries and refrain from applying measures which could adversely affect any of the forms of that co-operation;

— offer financial and other support to the programme of economic and technical co-operation among developed countries;
— provide resources through their aid programmes for the promotion of joint enterprises of developing countries through the financing of studies, technological research, evaluation of available technology, etc.
— give their support to all actions to be taken by international organizations with the aim of promoting economic and financial co-operation among developing countries.

During the UNCTAD meeting in Nairobi in May 1976 both the industrialized countries with so-called 'free market economies' and those with 'centrally planned economies' subscribed to the principle of the interdependence of nations and agreed that the prosperity of the international community as a whole depended upon the prosperity of all its constituent parts. But the Western industrialized countries qualified their support by saying that economic co-operation with the Third World depended upon the efforts of developing countries themselves.

In the second part we will look more closely at the international economic situation in order to see how Afro-Arab co-operation fits into an international context, and how far the developing countries can meet this challenge of the West, and demonstrate their ability to take co-ordinated action to help themselves.

PART II

THE NEW ECONOMIC ORDER

CHAPTER SEVEN

TRIANGULAR CO-OPERATION

It is extremely difficult for any country to break out of the international community. The white régimes in southern Africa, for example, have learnt this to their cost. What the leaders of Africa and the Arab States need to keep clear is that when they are formulating policies and guidelines for Afro-Arab co-operation they should take into account the interests of other members of the international community, particularly those of other countries of the Third World. The pattern of co-operation they establish should therefore relate to the new economic order.

The importance of international co-operation has been talked about for some time. As we saw above, in an attempt to reduce the gap between rich and poor nations the UN declared 1960-70 and 1970-80 to be Development Decades. The first was a failure. The second, which has been better planned, nevertheless looks as if it will have the same fate. The developing countries have tried to make the second decade a success, but the response of the developed countries has been disappointing. At both the 6th and 7th UN Special Sessions, developing countries called for change in the present international economic order. Their appeals were largely ignored. Outside of the formal sessions, representatives of the developed countries did in fact acknowledge the need to change the present order; but when pressed to define the time within which the change could take place, they were unwilling to be precise: some said it would not be within their lifetime; most were evasive.

An argument often used by representatives of the developed countries is to say that if the oil-exporting countries of the Third World had not plunged the international community into a serious economic crisis by substantially increasing the price of oil, their economies would have registered appreciable growth and this in turn would have stimulated demand for raw materials imported from countries of the Third World. It is true that the increase in the price of oil contributed to the present global recession. What it is not true to say is that all the economic ills are attributable to increases in the price of oil. The main causes of the present economic crisis are inherent in the economic systems of the industrialized countries themselves.

Another point which is often raised is that the developing countries receive substantial aid from the developed world. There has in fact, since 1959, been a demand for industrialized countries to contribute one per cent of their gross national product as aid to developing countries. The demand was first put forward at the International Confederation of Free Trade Unions' Sixth World Congress in Brussels when it adopted a statement appealing to all governments in advanced industrialized countries to increase substantially the flow of public capital funds into economically underdeveloped countries. They named one per cent of the national income as an indispensable minimum. This figure was taken up by the UN, and one of the objectives of the first Development Decade was that one per cent of the GNP of industrialized countries should be transferred to the Third World.

The most important traditional donor countries to economic development in Africa are members of the Development Assistance Committee (DAC) of the Organization for Economic Co-operation and Development (OECD). The OECD was originally formed to distribute Marshall Aid among European countries. In 1964 the member nations of DAC resolved to contribute one per cent of their gross national product to the development of the countries of the Third World, excluding underdeveloped Communist countries. This one per cent was to include both official Development Assistance (ODA) and private investment. When ODA and private investments were taken together, the contribution to the poor countries by the rich countries by early 1960 was nearly one per cent of the total GNP of the developing countries. By 1964 private investment was excluded from the calculation, and this made the target of one per cent too high. Table X gives some idea of ODA from DAC members as a percentage of the GNP of each donor country.

In 1975 ODA amounted to a total of $13.6 billion or 0.36%

of the total GNP of the DAC members concerned. What had actually happened was that the contribution of the Scandinavian countries, and of Australia, New Zealand and Canada had increased while that of some of the other members had declined. Assistance from the United States greatly exceeds that from any other country. A good deal of the aid from USA generally goes to countries of Asia and South America, and it is worth noting here that politics and not economics is the main criterion determining international flows of aid. North America's military allies often get especially large amounts of aid; the same is true of economic aid from the Soviet Union.

If we look at OPEC aid figures some surprising facts emerge. Before 1973 the Arab oil-exporting countries were unable to give appreciable aid to other Third World countries, because the price of oil was depressed and therefore the revenues were correspondingly low. This situation changed by 1974. During that year OPEC countries gave aid to the Third World amounting to $2.5 billion, representing 1.7% of their GNP. During the same period the developed countries of DAC contributed no more than 0.33% of their GNP. These figures exclude other forms of assistance. If all forms of assistance are taken into account we obtain the staggering figure of $6 billion from OPEC, representing 3.69% of the donors' GNP. During 1975 OPEC's total aid to the Third World was $9 billion which was 50% more than the previous year, whereas for the same period DAC countries' aid was only increased by about 15%.

What these figures bring out is that Arab oil-exporting countries are currently contributing a far greater share of their wealth to the development programmes of Third World countries than the Western industrialized nations. There is no doubt that Third World countries as a whole, and in particular countries of Asia, have benefitted from OPEC assistance. When aid is analysed according to regions, however, we find that in both relative and absolute terms Africa has received relatively little. Out of a net volume of $13,200 million in capital transfers to developing countries in 1973, only $438 million went to West Africa and $700 million to East Africa, making $1,138 million, which represents about 7% of the total

TABLE X

Flow of Official Development Assistance from Development Assistance Committee members measured as a percentage of Gross National Product[1]

	1960	1965	1970	1971	1972	1973	1974	1975	1976	1977	1978	1979	1980
Australia	.38	.53	.59	.53	.59	.44	.55	.61	.55	.56	.57	.57	.58
Austria		.11	.07	.07	.09	.15	.18	.17	.16	.16	.17	.17	.18
Belgium	.88	.60	.46	.50	.55	.51	.51	.59	.57	.61	.64	.65	.68
Canada	.19	.19	.42	.42	.47	.43	.50	.57	.58	.61	.65	.68	.70
Denmark	.09	.13	.38	.43	.45	.48	.55	.58	.62	.64	.67	.70	.70
Finland[2]		.02	.07	.12	.15	.16	.17	.18	.20	.22	.24	.27	.29
France	1.38	.76	.66	.66	.67	.58	.59	.62	.61	.59	.60	.61	.62
Germany	.31	.40	.32	.34	.31	.32	.37	.40	.32	.29	.28	.27	.26
Italy	.22	.10	.16	.18	.09	.14	.14	.11	.11	.12	.12	.12	.12
Japan	.24	.27	.23	.23	.21	.25	.25	.24	.23	.22	.22	.21	.20
Netherlands	.31	.36	.61	.58	.67	.54	.63	.75	.85	.88	.89	.88	.88
New Zealand[3]			.23	.23	.25	.27	.31	.52	.42	.41	.44	.46	.47
Norway	.11	.16	.32	.33	.43	.43	.57	.66	.74	.86	.96	.97	.97
Sweden	.05	.19	.38	.44	.48	.56	.72	.82	.86	.89	.92	.96	1.00
Switzerland	.04	.09	.15	.12	.21	.16	.15	.19	.16	.15	.14	.14	.14
United Kingdom	.56	.47	.37	.41	.39	.34	.38	.38	.37	.37	.39	.40	.41
United States[4]	.53	.49	.31	.32	.29	.23	.24	.27	.26	.24	.23	.22	.21

Grand Total													
ODA ($b-Nominal Prices	4.6	5.9	6.8	7.7	8.5	9.4	11.3	13.6	14.6	16.2	18.3	20.5	22.8
ODA ($b-Constant 1975 Prices)	11.0	12.3	11.5	12.2	12.1	11.6	12.7	13.6	13.6	14.1	14.6	15.3	15.9
GNP ($t-Nominal Prices)	.9	1.3	2.0	2.2	2.6	3.1	3.4	3.8	4.2	4.8	5.5	6.2	6.9
ODA as % GNP	.52	.44	.34	.35	.33	.30	.33	.36	.35	.34	.34	.33	.33
ODA Deflator[5]	.42	.48	.59	.63	.70	.81	.89	1.00	1.07	1.15	1.25	1.34	1.43

(1) Figures for 1975 and earlier years are based on actual data. Those for 1976-80 are based on OECD and World Bank estimates of growth of GNP, on information on budget appropriations for aid, and on aid policy statements by governments — they are projections, not predictions, of what will occur unless action, not now planned, takes place.
(2) Finland became a member of DAC in January 1975.
(3) New Zealand became member of DAC in 1973. ODA figures for New Zealand are not available for 1960 and 1965.
(4) In 1949, at the beginning of the Marshall Plan, US Official Development Assistance amounted to 2.79% of GNP.
(5) Includes the effect of parity changes. Figures through 1975 are based on DAC figures. Deflators for 1976-80 are the same as those for GNP.

Source: World Bank.

amount. India and other neighbouring Asian countries, on the other hand, received more aid than all the countries of Africa put together. How long Africa will continue to be forgotten in these capital transfers will depend upon the attitude of DAC and OPEC countries towards her. It is to be hoped that the strengthening of Afro-Arab co-operation will help to correct the balance.

One way of looking at the international community is to see it as a three-sided partnership. The industrialized countries can contribute technological expertise, the Arab countries have buying power and the African and other Third World countries possess enormous investment potential. Until recently, developed countries have had almost a complete monopoly of both technological and buying power. This is no longer the case, since there are now large sums of money in industrialized countries which belong to OPEC and which Western bankers only hold in trust. It is no secret that the partial loss of buying power is something the industrial countries are not happy about. What they are not yet willing to do is to see this as part of the necessary and long overdue redistribution of the world's resources. In this process, triangular co-operation will have an important role to play. The architects of this kind of co-operation will have to begin by bringing together technological and buying power and focusing them on one specific area, i.e. the Third World, in particular Africa. We have chosen Africa not for personal reasons, but because in Africa the development needs are great and the return on investment considerable. As many economists have observed, despite their immense mineral, agricultural and human resources the African economies have never really taken off. European technology is required to make the most of the geological, technical and economic potential of Africa. We have singled out Europe because of her industrial and technological strength and her traditional ties with Africa.

The Arab World, through financial institutions such as BADEA, has buying power which the Africans can utilize to bring industrial and technological power from Europe and America. It is extremely important for Africans and Arabs to assume an active role, and not stand by passively while the industrialized countries sell them technology and technicians. If Afro-Arab participation in the three-sided partnership is not dynamic and co-ordinated then Africa could become a dumping-ground for European market surpluses and technology. It could be the beginning of a new era of technological colonialism, brought about by Arab money, to the detriment of non-Arab African countries.

One of the problems standing in the way of the kind of three-sided co-operation we have been talking about is the lack of personal contact between Arabs and Africans. Successful co-operation requires a human touch; it cannot be managed and co-ordinated by remote control. There should be regular exchange visits not only for Heads of States, their Ministers and government officials, but also for scholars, businessmen, students and workers of Africa and the Arab World. We do not suggest that Arabs should come and live in Africa in great numbers, but they should at least have their own people on the spot to monitor the progress of the projects they finance. As far as publicity is concerned Arab embassies in Africa could also play an important role, but diplomats will never be a substitute for Arab technicians working directly with Africans. If Arabs were more often available to co-operate with their African counterparts, this would not only publicize Arab financial assistance to Africa but also advertise Afro-Arab solidarity to the world.

As well as contributing financial aid, Arab countries should try to ensure that some of their own people are engaged in the execution of the projects. In this way they can acquire up-to-date technological skills which are essential to their own development: it would constitute in-service training for Arab technical staff. For their part, African countries should be allowed to choose the fields and sectors where triangular co-operation could apply. All independent African States now have some kind of development plan with clearly identified priorities. In almost all of them infrastructure (such as roads, communications, education and rural development, with emphasis on food production and industry) is on top of the list. Clearly these are the areas in which Africans should encourage investment.

The third partner, the industrialized countries, should not be allowed to impose projects on Africa. It is not uncommon for industrial countries to export ill-suited technology to Africa in order to make profits. There is no point in triangular co-operation unless all three parties are committed to developing human and natural resources for the good of all mankind. Triangular co-operation should operate within the framework of a code of ethics agreed upon by all sides.

Within this triangular relationship Africa cannot of course depend solely on the financial resources of the Arab world. As we brought out in Chapter III, the Arab world also is in the process of development, and most of its income from oil needs to be ploughed back into its own economies. It is therefore necessary for Africa to find additional sources of funds for her economic development.

It is difficult to predict Africa's financial needs to 1980 with any degree of precision, both because of the absence of relevant data, and because of the large number of variable factors. Attempts have been made however, both by the World Bank and by the Dakar Club. These two institutions conduct their research independently, basing it on different assumptions and covering different periods. This probably accounts for many of the differences in their estimated figures.

The figures provided by the World Bank indicate that Africa's capital needs for medium and long-term development are US$3.5 billion per year for the period 1975-80. African countries who are members of OPEC (Algeria, Libya and Nigeria) have been excluded, but non-oil-producing Arab African countries such as Tunisia, Morocco, Egypt, Sudan and Mauritania have been included. In this forecast the following assumptions were made:

— average annual growth-rate of GNP, 6.5% during the period 1975-1980;
— average annual growth-rate of Western countries' GNP, 4% during the period 1975-1980;
— inflation rate for the same period, ranging between 4% and 6%;
— rate of increase in oil prices, approximately the same as that

of inflation.

The Dakar Club, consisting of African scholars from West Africa, was led by the Ivory Coast Minister of Planning, Mr Mohammed Diawara. Their studies covered the period between 1972 and 2000 and were based on West African economies. They estimated that West Africa alone would require US$114 billion, which amounts to US$4 billion per year. If these estimates are extended to the whole of Africa, we arrive at a staggering figure for the total capital requirements for the period under consideration. Yet if we take the World Bank figures as being more realistic, even their $3.5 billion is beyond the amount which can be raised from financial institutions within Africa. If the past disbursement of funds by the ADB is anything to go by, and if planned development in Africa has to depend on financial organizations of this kind, then it will never get off the ground. The ADB — which has a total capital of US$480 million — has so far in the last 12 years granted only $180 million to African countries, which averages out at US$15 million per year. According to IBRD estimates Africa requires about US$3 *billion*. There are, it is true, plans to increase ADB capital but even if they materialize there will still not be sufficient funds to meet the total needs of Africa. Table XI below shows the planned sources of revenue for ADB.

Even if we assume that the ADB is able to raise its working capital to US$400 million, this is still only on average US$80 million per year.

TABLE XI

Increase of Subscription	US $168.0 million
Government Loans	US $ 7.2 million
Stock bonds	US $ 15.0 million
Nigerian Trust Fund	US $ 60.0 million
Total	$250.2 million

Its subsidiary organization the ADF is in an even worse position. During 1975, the Fund had a target of US$90 million per year whereas it had projects requiring US$285 million in the pipeline. Despite the efforts of its officials it is unlikely that the gap between the revenue and expenditure of the ADF will be bridged between 1976 and 1980.

On the basis of projected revenue from both the ADB and the ADF Africa requires at least US$1 billion annually from other sources, even at an unrealistically conservative estimate.

It is difficult to arrive at a reasonable estimate of bilateral aid from OECD countries to Africa. This is because it is politically motivated and varies according to the support African countries give to the West particularly at the United Nations. Multilateral aid is channelled to Africa from Western industrialized countries through a) the World Bank, IDA and IFC, and b) the European Economic Community: Lomé Convention.

The International Bank for Reconstruction and Development (the World Bank), the International Development Agency (IDA) and the International Finance Corporation (IFC) all provide financial assistance to developing countries. The IBRD is a specialized Agency of the United Nations, while the IFC and the IDA are subsidiary organs of IBRD. IFC grants loans to private firms without necessarily requiring government guarantees. The IDA finances a certain range of projects to the least developed among developing countries on more concessionary terms than those of IBRD; of course the amounts involved are generally smaller than those given by IBRD.

The World Bank is one of the main international institutions from which capital is available for the development programmes of the Third World. IBRD by no means accepts all projects. Those projects which can attract private investment are as a rule rejected by the Bank. Another requirement is that the project for which a World Bank loan is sought must be sufficiently important to warrant a foreign exchange liability. The IBRD provides long term loans for periods not exceeding 25 years, but the interest rates charged cannot be described as concessionary because they take into account the cost of the money borrowed by the Bank plus one per cent commission and a quarter per cent administrative fee. In the mid-1970s the total interest charged was about 9%.

Between 1970 and 1975 the World Bank and IDA gave countries of Africa south of the Sahara US$2.8 billion. This was a great improvement on the previous five years (1965-70) when the amount given was US$1.2 billion. What are the prospects of the IBRD group in Africa during 1976-80? On the basis of approved loan programmes, the Bank and IDA have allocated a total of about US$6 billion to Africa for the five-year programme 1975-80, which comes to an average of US$1.2 billion per year. This is a remarkable improvement on the previous allocation. The agricultural sector will receive the greatest attention. The least developed countries of Africa will be allocated US$2 billion of the total amount allocated to Africa. Further breakdown will be as follows:

— West Africa: US$2.7 billion
— East Africa: US$3.2 billion

The sister organization, the International Monetary Fund, also offers financial assistance to countries of the Third World as well as to developed countries. The Fund helps member-countries to bridge short-term balance of payments deficits. African countries experiencing deficits in their balance of payments because of oil-price increases may seek assistance from the Fund through what is called the IMF Third Window programme. At the time of writing it is not yet known what proportion of the fund will go to Africa. In view of the good terms offered by the Third Window, any reasonable amount given to Africa will go a long way towards alleviating their balance of payment problems.

Parallel to World Bank aid is the EEC co-operation programme. On 28 February 1975, 46 countries of Africa, the Caribbean and the Pacific signed a Convention with the member-states of the European Economic Community. The Convention states that ACP countries will receive a grant from the European Community of 3.4 billion European units of account, which is approximately US$4 billion, for a period of five years from the date the Convention was signed. This works out to be an average of US$800 million per year. The negotiations had been going on for 18 months. At no time had the Community given any indication of the amount of aid which they were prepared to offer to ACP States. On the last day, in the early hours of the morning, they finally produced their figure, saying in effect, take it or leave it. However, the sum offered is unimpressive if we consider the tremendous resources of the member-states of the European Community. And the way in which it was proposed was unsatisfactory to Africans in that it was imposed rather than agreed upon. Representatives of ACP States refused to bargain on the offer from the Community; they simply made their disappointment known.

Table XII summarizes the financial requirement and known sources of aid for non-Arab African States based on the World Bank projections. From these figures we find that Africa's development budget for the period 1975-80 will have a deficit

TABLE XII

	$ million
Estimated Capital Requirement	15,000
Bilateral Aid	
France	500
Germany	600
Canada	600
	1,700
International Organizations	
IBRD and IDA	6,000
EEC	4,000
ADB and ADF	700
	10,700
Estimated revenue	12,400
Deficit	−2,600

of $2.6 billion, which gives an average annual deficit of about $500 million.

Of course, this is both a rough and conservative estimate. In order to implement the most urgent of her development projects, Africa requires at least $2.4 billion. Where is this to come from? If some of the Arab surpluses were to go into Africa, then Afro-Arab economic co-operation would start to become a reality. This would provide a sound basis for the kind of three-sided partnership with the industrialized nations that we have been proposing. If, in addition, the international community, through its economic and political organizations, were to adopt measures aimed at reducing the extent to which raw material producers are at the mercy of price fluctuations on the world market, then Africa's dependence on aid would diminish.

A step in this direction was taken at UNCTAD IV, held in Nairobi in May 1976. One of the resolutions to emerge was on the establishment of an integrated commodities programme. The principle was generally accepted by both the developed and developing countries. The integrated commodities programme resolution contained proposals about a raw materials policy, a list of commodities to be included in the programme, measures to be taken internally with regard to individual products, and the establishment of a common fund.

While accepting the general principle of an integrated commodities programme, the industrialized countries were reluctant to accept the principle of a common fund. They contended that the commodities under consideration had different characteristics and required different treatment: a uniform, global approach could not achieve the required objective. What they did not do was reject explicitly the establishment of a common fund, because they knew that such a course of action would lead to confrontation. Instead they proposed that the matter should be referred to the Secretary-General of UNCTAD who should convene conferences in which separate commodity agreements on individual products as well as the establishment of a common fund would be decided. In a spirit of good will and compromise the developing countries accepted these proposals.

It should be noted that although OPEC had supported the Group of 77 proposal to establish a common fund they were reluctant for the IMF to manage it because they considered it to be a conservative Western-dominated organization.

Advantages of an integrated commodities programme

1. An integrated approach would be cheaper, because at any given time some buffer-stocks would be selling while others would be buying. Some would be operating at a profit while others would be making losses, so central financing would spread the load, ease the cash flow and make individual disasters less likely.
2. Information available indicates that an integrated programme would give the widest possible area for trade-offs, i.e. Europe may not agree to deal on sugar, but they might be prepared to trade off sugar against a package of other commodities.
3. The dialogue which would be established as a result of the integrated approach would enable them to arrive at a price which would be fair and reasonable to the buyer and remunerative to the producer because there is often a price-supply figure for a commodity which both sides could meet.
4. The proposed stabilization schemes would not affect the industrialized countries unduly because their raw material imports only account for some 9% of their total import bill; furthermore, it will take time for the scheme to be operational, so the burden would be spread over a long period.

Problems with an integrated commodity programme

1. It is difficult to get agreement out of an organization as heterogeneous as UNCTAD, where there are more than 152 member countries whose interests have to be accommodated.
2. Overall cost: an integrated commodity programme could

not be realized without a common fund, and this would cost between \$6 billion and \$20 billion. According to the studies done by UNDP, copper alone would require a buffer stock of about 1% of a year's output. Other studies have revealed that copper would need \$2 billion out of \$6 billion proposed for the integrated package.

3. Pricing: with many commodities it is difficult to determine a good and sustainable price, which will be fair and reasonable to the buyers (developed countries) and fair and remunerative to the producers (developing countries). A remunerative price to the producer could lead to overproduction and overstocking of the buffer-stock, and lead buyers to react by switching to substitutes. The scheme would eventually break down, and this would have a bad effect on future programmes to be undertaken collectively by the world community. The United States and the Federal Republic of Germany have proposed the commodity-by-commodity approach. But this approach has been the foundation of all post-war efforts to deal with the commodity problem, and it has not produced the required results. It is therefore time to try the new techniques proposed in the integrated programme, i.e. the establishment of international stocks for a wide range of commodities, the creation of a common fund for financing such stock, multilateral trade commitments by governments on individual commodities, improved arrangements for the compensatory financing of fluctuations in prices and earnings, and the removal of trade barriers and other obstacles to the expansion of commodity processing in developing countries.

If the proposals to establish a common buffer-stock and a common fund for financing such stock become operational, the Federal Republic of Germany will be called upon by the international community to contribute more than any other member-state of the European Community. For this reason German opinion on the integrated programme and common fund is extremely important.

The West German Government has published an interesting paper on the advantages and disadvantages of the integrated commodities programme. The main purpose of the study was to show who stands to gain from the higher prices resulting from the stabilization of commodity prices. For the purpose of the study it was assumed that revenue from sales of 17 commodities (proposed by UNCTAD) would rise by ten per cent (on the basis of 1972 figures). This would lead to increased revenue of $2.7 billion from trade in these commodities. According to the study the three groups of the international community (developing, Western industrialized and Eastern socialist countries) would be affected as follows:

Developing countries, who export 54% and import 11% of the 17 commodities. Their revenue would rise by $1,409 million.

Western industrial countries, who export 29% and import 78% of the 17 commodities. They have a net loss of $1,439 million ($794 million in additional revenue, minus $2,233 million in additional import costs).

Eastern socialist countries (including the Peoples Republic of China), who export 7% and import 11% of the 17 commodities. Their net loss would be $128 million (in principle they supported the Integrated Programme at UNCTAD IV in Nairobi).

The authors of the report say that these global figures cover up the very different effects which the programme would have on individual countries. Of the Western industrial countries, six would stand to benefit — especially Australia (net gain $139 million) and South Africa (net gain $4 million). Most of the industrialized countries would record additional net costs — hardest hit would be Japan ($379 million) and the Federal Republic of Germany ($243 million). Of the Eastern Block countries, there would be a total net loss of $128 million while the Soviet Union would be the main 'winner'. What has not been taken into consideration is that, when the prices of primary commodities go up, the costs of finished products are also bound to go up. Countries like Japan and Germany, who according to the figures are supposed to come out the worst, would, in fact, through higher prices for finished products, pass on the costs of higher commodity prices to developing countries who buy from them.

In addition, most of the 17 commodities listed by UNCTAD for inclusion in the integrated commodities scheme are produced in large quantities by industrialized countries. If the prices of raw materials were increased, industrialized countries who produce these raw materials would reap maximum benefits. Since they process their own raw materials they can base their calculations for their finished products on the higher prices of raw materials. They would also have the option of charging prices lower than those prevailing in the international market and thereby have unfair advantage over those manufacturers who have to pay higher prices for their inputs of raw materials. The United States and some Eastern Socialist countries are likely to derive maximum benefit from this scheme.

It is clear from this that higher raw material prices will not necessarily succeed in distributing wealth more evenly among all nations of the globe. We venture to suggest, however, that indexing the prices of primary commodities to those of industrial goods would at least ensure that developing countries are able to cover the production costs of their raw materials and make reasonable profits to be used in the acquisition of additional plant and machinery in order to increase volume of production.

It is sometimes argued that the integrated commodities scheme could not be accepted by the industrialized countries in its present form because it contains too many planned-economy elements. The purchasing and supply obligations inherent in the scheme are at variance with a market economy. The multiplicity of commodity agreements with long-term price fixing would lead to distortions in the world economy which will not be in the economic interests of either the industrialized or the developing countries. One answer to this is to have an integrated commodities programme with commodity agreements and buffer stocks without a common fund. For each commodity there would be an upper and lower limit. If the price fluctuated outside these limits over a long period, the price band would have to be shifted correspondingly. Such a phase-flexible arrangement would equitably meet the interests of both producer and consumer countries. The main preoccupation of the developing countries is not to impose a particular system but to ensure that the price they receive for their products is fair and reasonable.

The integrated commodities programme is of particular importance to Africa. Most African countries depend on one single commodity. Table XIII shows the percentage of overall export earnings from the most important commodity of selected developing countries in 1974. It is important to note that the dependence on commodity export is greater in the economically most disadvantaged countries.

TABLE XIII

Country	Percentage	Commodity
Burundi	84.3	Coffee
Chad	67.2	Cotton
Liberia	65.5	Iron ore
Mauritania	71.5	Iron ore
Rwanda	62.0	Coffee
Togo	76.4	Phosphate
Uganda	72.7	Coffee
Zaire	73.2	Copper ore
Zambia	92.7	Copper ore

The Arabs could assist Africa by using their newly acquired influence to support the integrated commodities programme. If they were to contribute to the proposed Common Fund it would be a very positive step towards co-operation with Africa, since most non-Arab African countries depend on their commodities for export earnings which are essential to finance their development. More important than this, however, is that it would constitute a way of helping Africa to help herself. Afro-Arab solidarity within an international framework could result in a more equal and mutually beneficial Afro-Arab partnership.

CHAPTER EIGHT

THE NORTH-SOUTH DIALOGUE

Throughout this book we have emphasized the importance of contact between Arabs and Africans. We have at the same time tried to give some idea of the problems and difficulties that the Afro-Arab dialogue can and does run into. When it comes to broader international debate, these problems of dialogue seem to be greatly accentuated. The recent Conference on International Economic Co-operation, which became known as the North-South Dialogue, certainly bears this out.

The North-South Dialogue has its roots in the United Nations. Since 1970, the international community has witnessed instability in the international monetary situation, world inflation, an energy crisis and finally global economic recession. These crises brought home the important fact that in order to find permanent solutions to these problems the peoples of the world must learn to work together in a spirit of co-operation. In this regard the North-South Dialogue can be seen as an attempt to achieve international co-operation in order to establish an economic order more in keeping with present day reality.

The first call for a new international economic order was made at the conference of non-aligned nations in Algiers in September 1973. Then, in the spring of 1974, a special session of the United Nations General Assembly was convened at the request of Algeria. At this session the Third World leaders called upon the developed world to co-operate with them in their efforts to strengthen the economies of their countries. Although there was no direct or immediate response from the leaders of the developed countries, it is fair to say that they were at least prepared to listen to the call made by the countries of the Third World.

The first positive step was taken at the Seventh Special Session of the UN General Assembly when an initial dialogue was established between the developing world and the developed world on the questions of the new order. This session was characterized by an atmosphere of good will. Both sides recognized that confrontation is not generally productive, with the result that they were willing to look for areas of possible co-operation. The Algerian Foreign Minister, Abdelaziz Bouteflika, who was President of this special session, stated that it had become clear that much of the prosperity of the West is derived from the draining of the wealth of the people of the Third World, and the exploitation of their labour. He noted with satisfaction that in the international community there is now an awareness of the fact that all nations are interdependent and that it is no longer possible for any one nation to impose individual solutions to global problems. He went on to pose pertinent and provocative questions. What kind of world do we want to build? What kind of future are we preparing for the coming generations? He called on the developed countries to demonstrate their will to co-operate with developing countries. In such new relationships, he said, the first step was for the more fortunate nations to make the necessary concessions and to yield to the legitimate aspirations of those to whom history — and sometimes nature too — has been ungenerous.

During this special session the UN Secretary-General Kurt Waldheim took a very active part in the debate. In order to attain the objective of establishing a New World Economic Order he proposed the following lines of action:

— First, through the General Assembly, the United Nations should provide the blueprint, framework and guidelines for the negotiating process which will ensue both within and outside the United Nations system.

— Second, the results of these negotiations should be brought before the General Assembly in order to give such agreements the confirmation which only a universal organization can provide.

— Finally, the United Nations can provide continuity by monitoring and following up agreements reached by the international community.

The friendly atmosphere of the Seventh Special Session was summed up by the representatives of Mauritius, who said that, 'unlike any previous debate this particular one is like a genuine conversation between nations.' It is important to note that there was nothing particularly new at either the Sixth or the Seventh Sessions. The issues were well known by both parties; what was new was the conciliatory attitudes of both the developed and the developing countries.

The North-South Dialogue was a product of the UN General Assembly at its Seventh Session. It was in fact originally intended to be a conference between the Western industrialized countries and OPEC. This was an idea of Dr Kissinger's which he tried to sell to other industrialized countries, including Japan, Australia and New Zealand. It was in line with the US decision to organize an International Energy Agency as a counter-weight to OPEC. The French President, Giscard d'Estaing, did not want a confrontation with OPEC. He considered the US proposal as a 'war machine' against oil producers. Instead he made alternative proposals. He suggested holding an international conference on energy, with a larger membership including oil producers, industrialized countries and non-oil-producing countries of the Third World.

With this objective in mind France convened a meeting in Paris on 7 April 1975, to which were invited Algeria, Saudi Arabia, the EEC countries, the US, India, Iran, Japan, Venezuela and Zaire. The US and other industrialized countries accepted the principle of the conference on the understanding that it be based on finding a ceiling price for oil as proposed by Dr Kissinger. The meeting did not produce the desired results because of fundamental disagreement among participants as to the aims of the conference. Arab participants were concerned about the economic plight of African developing countries and insisted that the Conference should deal with the problems of raw materials and economic development. Algeria was the champion of this proposal. But the developed countries, under the aegis of the US, wanted the Conference to concentrate on energy problems exclusively. After protracted negotiations a compromise was reached on the issues to be discussed and in mid-October 1975 the title was changed to the Conference on International Economic Co-operation.

In December 1975, a ministerial meeting of the CIEC was

convened in Paris. It was attended by Foreign Ministers or Senior Ministers of the 27 participating states. The US Delegation was led by Secretary of State, Dr Kissinger.

The Conference was divided into two groups. The industrialized countries (or Group of 8) included the EEC Commission, Australia, Canada, Spain, the USA, Japan, Sweden and Switzerland. The developing countries (or Group of 19) included both oil-producing countries — Algeria, Indonesia, Iraq, Iran, Nigeria, Saudi Arabia and Venezuela — and non-oil-producing countries — Argentina, Brazil, Cameroon, Egypt, India, Jamaica, Mexico, Pakistan, Peru, Yugoslavia, Zaire and Zambia. The conference was chaired by two co-chairmen — Mr Allen MacEachen, the Canadian Minister of Foreign Affairs, designated by the OECD, and his Venezuelan counterpart Mr Manuel Perez Guerrero, nominated by the Group of 77.

The Group of 77 both at the United Nations in New York and at UNCTAD in Geneva had expressed the view that the developing countries who were not represented at the Paris Conference would only benefit if the OPEC countries who dominated the Group of 19 delegation were to use their newly acquired oil power to persuade the Group of 8 to accept meaningful changes in the economic structure of oil.

The leadership of the four Commissions was as follows: the Energy Commission was headed by two co-chairmen from Saudi Arabia and the US; the Raw Materials Commission was chaired by Japan and Peru; the Development Commission was presided over by Algeria and the EEC; and the Finance Commission was looked after by Iran and the EEC. Each Commission had 15 members, ten from developing countries. The conference needed technical expertise, so they drew upon the experience of a number of international organizations which were invited to join in the Commissions' deliberations, but did not have the right to vote. These were the UN, OPEC, the International Energy Agency, UNCTAD, OECD, FAO, GATT, UNIDO, IMF, IBRD, the Latin American Economic System and the UN Development Programme.

Politicians and economists alike, particularly those who were not represented at the Paris Conference, were sceptical about the outcome of the North-South Dialogue. There was one school of thought which believed that the conference was no more than a duplication of UNCTAD. Others considered it to be a tactical move on the part of the Western industrialized countries to involve the developing countries (Group of 77) in permanent dialogue. Some even believed that the Paris Conference was simply a French manoeuvre to gain international prestige.

The question of whether the CIEC and UNCTAD differ in any significant way is a difficult one. There are certainly marked differences of approach, but the fact that neither has met with much success would seem to suggest that these differences are outweighed by their underlying similarities.

Some economists and politicians have argued that the CIEC is a rival of UNCTAD, and that this contributed in some way to the failure of UNCTAD IV in Nairobi. They claimed that if Western industrialized countries were going to give concessions then they preferred to do so in CIEC rather than UNCTAD. This argument would have more weight if UNCTAD was not already well-known for its record of failures. In 1962, 1964 and 1972 UNCTAD had postponed most of the major issues, so it is scarcely surprising that UNCTAD IV was influenced by this. The failure of UNCTAD IV was clear from early on. The Board of UNCTAD, meeting in Geneva prior to the conference, was charged with the responsibility of resolving all technical issues leaving only policy matters to be referred to the ministerial meeting in Nairobi. Instead of doing this the Board spent two weeks getting nowhere. Industrialized countries refused to give positive reactions to concrete proposals submitted by developing countries. When pressed for a specific reply they said that the purpose of the Board meeting was simply to exchange views because they had no political mandate to commit their governments.

In spite of this, the developing countries at the Paris Conference did what they could to ensure that UNCTAD IV was a success. Just before the meeting in Nairobi in May 1976 the Group of 19 issued a statement which was intended to warn the industrialized countries that unless there were tangible results at the Nairobi Conference there was no point in continuing with the dialogue in Paris. Part of the statement read as follows:

> 'UNCTAD IV constitutes the first international meeting of a universal character where the members of the international community will be called upon to demonstrate their political determination to attain their common goals of establishing a new international economic order. The Group of 19 expected the discussions at CIEC would lay down the foundations for future proceedings. However, after submitting concrete proposals in various fields in order to reach the CIEC aims and not having received up to now any positive reactions or constructive counter proposals, the Group of 19 expresses its dissatisfaction at the slowness of the progress at the Paris Conference. This is due principally to the lack of political will on the part of some developed countries. The Group is convinced that unless substantial results are achieved at UNCTAD IV the future of the CIEC dialogue will be compromised.'

This statement is in line with the indignation shown by the Group of 19 at the close of the CIEC Third Session. 'If we continue at this rate,' warned the President of the Group of 19, Mr Perez Guerrero, at a Press Conference, 'we shall get nowhere.' His statement was in marked contrast to that of Mr Bosworth, Co-Chairman of the Energy Commission and leader of the American delegation. He said that the progress achieved on the Commission level was encouraging and would be useful to the Nairobi meeting of UNCTAD. The Japanese delegation, who invariably support the US position, said that the proposals of the developing countries were ambiguous and needed further clarification.

There is no way the work done during the major part of the conference could be described as a success. The main cause of the failure stemmed from the fact that the representatives of the Group of 8 were not willing to negotiate on substantive issues such as the establishment of a common fund for financing buffer-stocks under the integrated commodities programme; the price indexing of raw materials from the

Third World against manufactured imports from the industrialized countries; the stabilization of the export earnings of developing countries, including compensation for loss of earnings arising from fluctuations in the price of their raw materials; the lowering, and in some cases abolition, of prohibitive tariffs on manufacturers from the Third World; and the transfer of technology from the developed to the developing countries.

There was one very striking difference between the attitudes of the developed and the developing countries. Whereas the developing countries invariably presented a united front, the other group appeared to maintain their individual positions on almost all issues which were before the conference. Their comments clearly demonstrated that they were expressing the views not of a group, but of their respective countries. This approach made the work of the conference unmanageable. It became nothing more than a forum where people came to give the views of their different governments. The developing countries had come to Paris because they sincerely believed that it was going to be an economic conference at which important decisions would be made to change the old economic structure. What actually happened was that it turned out to be a political conference rather than an economic one.

DISAGREEMENTS IN PARIS

On 30 May 1977 the long-awaited Ministerial conference was finally convened. Almost all member-States of the conference were represented by a senior Minister. These included the American Secretary of State, Cyrus Vance, the German Foreign Minister, Rudi Genscher, and the British Foreign Secretary, David Owen.

The meeting was formally opened by De Guiringaud, the French Minister of Foreign Affairs. He recalled that when the Ministers met for the first time in December 1975 a mighty task awaited them. A vast field of investigations was opened up to them. Their task was to gain a clear insight, in the field of energy, raw materials and development, into the increasing interdependence of their economies, and to identify technical and financial solutions aimed at securing both the growth of the Third World and the establishment of more mutually beneficial relations between all partners of an economic order which is henceforth vital to mankind as a whole. The decisions to be reached by the conference would affect the lives of hundreds of millions of people living in an appalling state of destitution. The world was confident that the Ministers assembled had the ability to introduce a greater measure of rationality and equity into the relations between developing and industrialized countries. It was believed that compromises were needed to ensure the success of the conference, where the Ministers were expected to make decisions in energy, raw materials, development and finance.

Energy. The Commission on Energy submitted its report to the Ministerial meeting. It had been able to arrive at a common text for the major portion of the final report, but there were areas of divergence on the questions of energy prices, access to markets and assurances of energy supply. In the following paragraphs we shall attempt a broad description of the areas of divergence and the areas of agreement.

Both sides agreed that the availability and supply of energy resources should make commercial sense and take into account technical limitations, financial needs, and other constraints. The industrialized countries refused to accept the additional formulation submitted by the developing countries that any arrangements made must also take into account future requirements of countries currently exporting energy.

There was no disagreement regarding the need to have adequate and stable supplies of energy, both non-renewable and renewable, to ensure the economic well-being and progress of all countries. It was agreed, however, that all countries will need to contribute on the basis of their individual capacities and potential.

With regard to the transfer of technology relating to extraction of energy there was a general agreement regarding the principle itself but there was disagreement on the methods of its implementation. The developing oil-exporting countries contended that those countries in possession both of sources of energy other than oil and gas and of the necessary technology to develop such energy sources should undertake to provide both, on a stable and non-discriminating basis, to countries which require them for supply or diversification purposes. The industrialized countries refused to accept this proposal. They recognized the need to facilitate access to technology on a non-discriminatory basis; but they argued that it should be done through appropriate means of international co-operation in accordance with appropriate national and international standards. They further stated that the patents of Western technology are owned by the *companies* responsible — they are not owned by *governments*, as would be the case with most developing countries. The industrialized countries therefore refused to enact legislation which would be at variance with the operations of a free market existing in their respective countries.

Both sides agreed that oil-exporting developing countries need to be assisted in diversifying their economic base in order to fulfil their development plans and sustain their long-term economic progress (an integral part of such diversification for these developing countries is the progressive expansion of downstream hydro-carbon processing). And both sides recognized the limited grasp in all countries of the world's energy, economic and monetary prospects. They would all benefit from improved knowledge in these fields.

There was general agreement that the Law of the Sea Conference should continue its efforts to establish, in accordance with the principle of the common heritage of mankind, an international programme for the exploitation of the natural or mineral resources of the deep-sea bed area beyond the limits of national jurisdiction; and to ensure equitable sharing by states in the benefits derived therefrom, taking into particular consideration the interests and needs of developing countries, as provided for in Resolution 2769 (XXV) of the UN General Assembly.

The Ministerial meeting was unable to reach agreement on a recommendation for the issue of accumulated revenues from oil exports. It was therefore decided that the conference should merely take note of the situation for further consideration in other appropriate forums.

There was general agreement on measures to be taken for effective energy co-operation between developed and developing countries. They urged other international and regional financial institutions to consider the role they might play in contributing to greater capital flows to developing countries, particularly energy-importing developing countries, for energy development.

The conference made little of the question of energy because the parties concerned could not agree on the fundamental issues, particularly energy prices. The conference considered various proposals submitted by delegations for recommendations on the issues of energy prices and the purchasing power of energy export earnings, and was unable to reach agreement on them. Even on measures on which there was some agreement, the parties failed to agree on the best possible method of implementation. The developing countries proposed that the implementing of the agreed conclusions and recommendations be carried out by the governments of the respective countries, with due regard to the linkage between energy problems and those of raw materials, development and finance. The contrary view of the developed countries was that measures agreed upon would involve various forms of contact amongst energy-exporting and energy-importing countries both developed and developing. The possibility of establishing institutional arrangements to facilitate this contact and continue consultation on energy issues remains to be considered in other appropriate forums.

Raw Materials. On the question of local processing and diversification, the conference agreed that appropriate institutions covering commodity arrangements should, through funds and other measures, foster research and development activities, the improvement of marketing and of the technical characteristics of processed products, the development of raw materials, and the adapting of imported processing technology to the local conditions of developing countries. Developing countries submitted that commodity agreements should include commitments from developed countries to import from developing countries increasing quantities of commodities in their processed and semi-processed form. This was not accepted by the developed countries.

The biggest surprise the developed countries gave to the developing countries was their acceptance of the establishment of the Common Fund as an integral part of the integrated programme. They qualified this by stating that the Common Fund should be operated in conjunction with individual funds for specific commodities, but it was still a big breakthrough. The Western industrialized countries had rejected the idea of a Common Fund when it was first mooted by UNCTAD Secretariat — indeed, the idea almost marked the end of UNCTAD. In Nairobi, when Western countries led by the US and the Federal Republic of Germany rejected the concept of a Common Fund, the developing countries were prepared to go it alone. The Secretary-General of UNCTAD saved the situation by proposing a workable compromise which was accepted by the conference: the negotiations were to continue in Geneva, by the UNCTAD Board of Governors. Certainly, the acceptance of the Common Fund by the Western industrialized countries was the best news to come from North-South Dialogue.

As a general principle the conference agreed that special attention should be given to both the short-term and the long-term problems faced by developing countries which depend on growing imports of raw materials and foodstuffs as an essential element of continued economic growth. The developed countries stressed the importance of assisting the least developed among importing developing countries. Developing countries wanted a general provision — protecting not only the least developed and most seriously affected countries but also those lacking in natural resources — to be borne in mind when implementing the Integrated Programme.

There was general agreement that developing countries should be allowed to play a greater part in the transport, marketing and distribution of their raw materials. The developed countries singled out Africa as a continent which needed special assistance to enable her to develop her infrastructure, particularly transportation. The following were specific agreements:

1. (a) The developed countries and specialized international or regional organizations should intensify their efforts to provide aid and technical assistance programmes.
   (b) Efforts should be made to promote the international exchange of information on supply, demand and trade in raw materials and its dissemination down to the individual producers.
   (c) Governments should facilitate or assist efforts by individual or joint commercial enterprises of developing countries to establish marketing operations in developed countries.
2. Developed and developing countries should contribute actively to the elaboration of a mutually acceptable code of conduct by the United Nations Commission on Trans-national Corporations — with a view to its timely adoption.
3. Barriers to fair competition between marketing enterprises of developed and developing countries should be eliminated.
4. Action must be taken to improve the functioning of commodity exchanges dealing with products exported by developing countries and promotional measures in this direction.
5. International institutions are to be encouraged to extend advice, technical assistance or other appropriate support to developing countries interested in setting up in their own territories commodity exchanges dealing with their export commodities.

The Conference failed to resolve the issue of a code of conduct for trans-nationals. The developed countries refused to accept the point of view of developing countries. Disagreement arose on the following issues:

1. Re-affirmation of the right of developing countries to take action, whether individually or collectively, with a view to counterbalancing the predominant position of trans-national corporations in the determination of international prices of commodities. Developed countries were requested to undertake not to retaliate against such actions.
2. The question whether or not the code of conduct for trans-

nationals should be legally binding.

3. The question of a code of conduct for conference lines.

On the question of provision of technical and financial assistance aimed at increasing the share of developing countries in world shipping tonnage and trade, developed countries gave a negative response.

There was a general recognition of the importance to the economic and social development of certain developing countries of earnings from exports of natural products subject to competition from synthetic products. Developing countries urged developed countries to regulate and control production of synthetics which compete with natural products, particularly those synthetics that have a great capacity for pollution. Developed countries argued that the obligation was mutual.

The conference participants recognized the importance of the question of the purchasing power of developing countries. It was agreed that the issue could be approached by looking at the scope for an improvement in the export earnings of the countries concerned, enabling them to achieve the economic and social development essential to them. There was agreement that the long-term solution for continued and equitable growth in the world economy lay mainly in the local processing of the raw materials and in the establishment of manufacturing industries in the developing countries, permitting, *inter alia*, adequate market access to the developed countries by eliminating or reducing tariff and non-tariff barriers.

Development and Finance. On the question of indebtedness of developing countries, no agreement was reached because of fundamental conceptual differences. Developed countries drew a distinction between the structural problems of countries dependent largely on aid, and the crises arising from debt. They said that in acute debt-crisis situations where a debtor country faces a default or imminent default, the 'creditor club' will carry out debt reorganization operations on the basis of features of past debt negotiations. In the case of structural problems of a longer-term nature, where an adverse structure of the balance of payments hampers development, at the request of the recipient concerned the case would be dealt with expeditiously in an appropriate forum on an individual basis with a view to providing aid. Developing countries were of the view that international action should be taken at an early stage of emerging debt problems and not when indebtedness reaches crisis proportions.

Developed countries rejected a proposal from the developing countries for an extraordinary and one-shot operation of relief on official debts. They submitted that such relief should consist of the withdrawal of the outstanding debts, or, in some cases, in its re-computation at IDA terms. It is fair to say that on the question of indebtedness of developing countries, industrialized countries were adamant and unco-operative in the extreme. Developing countries were disillusioned and decided not to press any further.

Developed countries were more co-operative on the question of foreign direct investment. Some delegates of developing countries believed that industrialized countries were keen on the subject of foreign investments because they wanted to increase their foreign markets and their spheres of economic influence. Foreign investments are usually returned as capital repayment plus interest or profit. There was a general agreement on the desirability of establishing a suitable framework to encourage and facilitate foreign investment and its harmonious integration and contribution to the development plans and policies of host countries.

Agreements were reached regarding developing countries' access to capital markets. Both sides pledged to support any efforts to expand this access.

It was recognized that to some developing countries official development assistance was vital for their economic development. But the conference also noted that the primary responsibility for the economic development of the developing countries rests with the developing countries concerned. They are determined to make every effort to solve their problems, and to carry out the necessary improvements in their economic and social structures. Outside assistance should complement their own internal efforts.

Developed countries showed a commendable spirit of good

will. They voluntarily offered to provide food assistance to countries afflicted by drought and other natural disasters which disrupt normal planting and harvesting arrangements. In concerted effort they formulated solutions to the world food problem, including such issues as malnutrition and the improvement of agriculture. They agreed that the minimum 4% annual growth-rate in agriculture and food production in developing countries, agreed at the world conference, could be achieved only through the investment of concerted efforts and resources by developing and developed countries and appropriate international institutions.

They recognized that in this area the developing countries concerned cannot help themselves. There is, therefore, a need for bilateral donors, multilateral aid agencies and institutions to increase effectively and substantially their official development assistance to agriculture and food production in developing countries.

The conference was delighted to learn of the attainment of the agreed target of $1 billion as the contribution to the initial sources of IFAD (International Fund for Agricultural Development), as supported by the Development Commission. There was a general agreement that every effort should be made to expand the supply and production of fertilizers in the developing countries. In most developing countries where there is a food shortage, either the climatic conditions are unfavourable to agriculture or there is an acute chemical deficiency in the soil. Insects can also be a menace to the crops. It is therefore essential to increase production capacities and supplies of pesticides in developing countries through financial and technical assistance by donor countries.

The conference called upon the competent body, the FAO, to make an early decision for undertaking formal negotiations leading to the conclusion of a new international grains agreement, which should pay particular attention to safeguarding the special interests of the developing countries and should contain the important provisions regarding the international system of nationally held reserves. The principle regarding the creation of a minimum safe carry-over level of stocks was accepted, but there was no agreement regarding a specific minimum *percentage* safe carry-over level of stocks. Developing countries had proposed a level of stocks of 17% to 18% of world annual cereal consumption, as estimated by the FAO Committee on World Food Security, as a reasonable level to protect the world against well-defined exigencies and minimize fluctuations in grain prices. Developed countries said that studies done so far were inadequate and therefore could not be used as a basis for determining the minimum safe carry-over level of stocks. They called for further research into the matter. They also emphasized that any studies done in this respect should not be construed to imply any particular commitment as regards the level of stocks to be adopted in an international agreement on cereals.

The conference used the language of the World Food Conference in Rome in 1975. They called on all governments able to furnish external assistance to increase substantially their official development assistance to agriculture in developing countries, especially the least developed and the most seriously affected countries, including capital assistance on soft terms, transfer of appropriate technology and programme loans for imports of essential inputs. A request was also made to the World Bank, Regional Banks, the United Nations Development Programme, the Food and Agriculture Organization of the United Nations, the United Nations Industrial Development Organization and other international agencies, through modification of their existing policies as appropriate, to increase substantially their assistance for agriculture and fisheries in developing countries.

The conference recognised that in the past there had been undue delay in the disbursement of funds earmarked for agricultural products of needy countries because of cumbersome and often out-moded procedures. In this regard the conference urged international and regional organizations to simplify and streamline the procedures for granting such assistance. They also sought support from the UN itself and its agencies to mobilize the support of the entire international community, for the urgent task of overcoming hunger and malnutrition.

Although the conference failed to reach agreement on other

equally important matters, satisfactory decisions were made on issues relating to food and agriculture.

At last, on 4 June 1977, the protracted negotiations came to a close. The delegates agreed that the United Nations General Assembly should take up issues which had not been resolved and transfer them to competent bodies either for implementation or for further dialogue. At the end of the day consensus emerged that the postponement of the Ministerial Meeting in December (mainly due to the unpreparedness of the new Carter administration in Washington) was a blessing in disguise. If the meeting had taken place in December as planned, it would have been doomed to fail. The political climate was not ripe for such a crucial gathering. There was no political goodwill on the part of the industrialized countries who were being asked to give up their entrenched privileges.

The Summit in May 1977 in London of the most affluent Western industrialized countries — the US, Canada, the UK, France, Italy, West Germany and Japan — came up with encouraging statements regarding the restructuring of the world economy. Declarations made by these materially powerful leaders seemed to indicate a new approach by Western industrialized countries to the problems of development of developing countries. The developing countries, even given all the goodwill in the air, did not expect the complex world to change overnight; but they had expected more to happen at the Paris Conference.

Although the conference was not a success in the truest sense of the word, it is fair to say that the eighteen months spent on it were fruitful. A lot of work had been done to facilitate future meetings dealing with the restructuring of the global economy. As stated in previous paragraphs some decisions simply await implementation.

Those who have not been party to these negotiations will be disappointed with the outcome of the Paris Conference, particularly those whose negotiations in their own forums had to be postponed. In terms of concrete results the conference was certainly lacking, but one hopes that, when the proceedings are made available to UNCTAD in Geneva and to the United

Nations General Assembly, those forums which had postponed their negotiations will benefit from the substance of the negotiations in the Paris Conference. The main stumbling-block at the Paris negotiations was that each side felt that there were certain principles on which they could not compromise. As one negotiator put it: 'Certain compromises would negate the purpose for which we are here — to restructure the present system which has worked to our disadvantage.'

The North-South Dialogue has taught us one important lesson: the establishment of a new economic order has to involve the West in giving up a certain amount of the privilege it has enjoyed for many years at the expense of the rest of the world. It is never easy to relinquish privilege, and, knowing that, it would be unrealistic for us to expect rapid success. But we can take heart from the excellent relations between the African and Arab delegates at the Paris Conference. They have collaborated on all issues which have come up during the conference and have supported each other on matters both of mutual and individual interest. Economic change is going to depend on the amount of pressure which the developing world can exert upon the developed countries. The Arab oil-exporting group is now in a position to exert pressure: what is positive about their solidarity with other developing countries is that the pressure they are beginning to exert may eventually become more widely beneficial.

APPENDIX

Declaration and Action Programme for African-Arab Co-operation

In Cairo on 9 March 1977, the first Arab-African Summit Conference affirmed its determination to develop, deepen and expand the horizons and fields of co-operation among the African states and the Arab world, to strengthen the existing ties between their peoples proceeding from the joint and several interests and ties between the two sides, from the geographical, historical and cultural considerations linking them and from the requirements of their joint struggle against all forms of domination and exploitation.

This was contained in the Declaration and Action Programme for African-Arab co-operation which was issued at the end of the Conference. The two sides reaffirmed their support for the African and Arab questions and their condemnation of imperialism, colonialism, neo-colonialism, Zionism and racial and religious discrimination, particularly in Africa, Palestine and in the occupied Arab territories.

Following is the text of the Declaration and Action Programme on Arab-African co-operation:

INTRODUCTION

1. We, the kings and heads of states and governments, members of the OAU and the Arab League, meeting in Cairo from 7 to 9 March 1977;

2. Taking into consideration the OAU Charter and the Arab League Charter;

3. Noting the resolutions and decisions issued at various levels, especially those issued by the 8th extraordinary session and the 23rd and 24th ordinary sessions of the OAU, by the 6th and 7th Arab Summit Conferences, and by the 62nd and 63rd ordinary sessions of the Arab League, in consolidation of co-operation among states;

4. Aware of our numerous links and interests, of the

geographical, historical and cultural factors, of the desire to develop co-operation in the political, economic and social spheres, and of the requirements of our joint struggle against all kinds of domination and exploitation;

5. Appreciating the bonds of friendship, fraternity, and good neighbourliness between the African and Arab states;

6. Prompted by a common will to strengthen the understanding between our peoples and the co-operation between our states in fulfilment of our peoples' aspiration to stronger Arab-African fraternity;

7. Determined to strengthen the existing links between our states and peoples by setting up joint organizations;

8. Taking into consideration the common interests and ambitions of the African and Arab peoples;

9. Convinced that Arab-African co-operation falls within the context of the joint action of all the developing states for the sake of further co-operation, and for the sake of intensifying their efforts to promote a new international economic system that will be more fair and more just;

10. Determined to use our natural resources and manpower for the overall progress of our peoples in all walks of human activity;

11. Noting the principles and provisions of the Algiers charter, the Lima declaration and the African declaration on co-operation, development and economic independence; of the declarations, resolutions, and action programme for economic co-operation issued by the 4th summit conference of non-aligned states; of the economic provisions relating to the liquidation of imperialism included in the declaration of the Islamic summit conference in Lahore; of the official declaration of the summit conference of the OPEC kings and heads of state; of the declaration and programme of work for the promotion of a new international economic system issued by the sixth special session of the UN General Assembly; of the charter of economic rights and duties of states; and of the

declaration of action programme issued by the Dakar conference on raw materials and development;

12. Have approved this Declaration and Action Programme defining the principles and framework of Arab-African collective and individual efforts in the field of Arab-African co-operation.

THE PRINCIPLES

13. The political and economic co-operation between the African and Arab states is particularly based on the following principles: (a) respect for the sovereignty of all our states, their safety, the unity of their lands and their political independence; (b) equality among all the states; (c) permanent sovereignty of the states and the peoples over their natural resources; (d) the shunning of aggression and the illegality of the forcible occupation or annexation of the land of others; (e) non-interference in the domestic affairs of the other states; (f) the preservation of mutual interests on the basis of reciprocal treatment and equality; (g) the settlement of differences and the resolving of disputes peaceably and in a spirit of tolerance; (h) the joint struggle against hegemony, racialism and exploitation in all their forms in order to preserve international peace and security.

CO-OPERATION FIELDS AND THE ACTION PROGRAMME

A — Co-operation fields

14. The African and Arab countries pledge to develop their relations on the bilateral and multilateral levels on the basis of a comprehensive and long-term co-operation in the following fields: (a) political and diplomatic; (b) economic and financial; (c) trade; (d) education, culture, science, technology and information.

B — Political and diplomatic co-operation

15. The African and Arab countries again reaffirm their commitment to the policy of non-alignment as an important

factor in the struggle for: (a) the freedom and independence of the nations; (b) the establishment of a world in which peace and security for all states prevail; (c) the comprehensive application of the principles of peaceful coexistence; (d) colouring international relations with a democratic tint; (e) equal rights in co-operation; (f) economic development.

16. The Arab and African countries condemn imperialism, colonialism, neo-colonialism, Zionism, racial segregation and all forms of racial and religious discrimination and apartheid, particularly in Africa, Palestine, and the occupied Arab territories.

17. The Arab and African countries reaffirm their support for the African and Arab issues and pledge to co-ordinate their actions in the international sphere, particularly in the United Nations on matters of common interest. In order to achieve this, the African and Arab groups in international organizations will establish closer co-operation.

18. The two sides will continue to extend their political, diplomatic, financial and moral support to the African and Arab national liberation movements recognized by the OAU and the Arab League.

19. The member states of the two sides will exert efforts to establish and strengthen their diplomatic and economic representation in each other's countries and will strengthen the contacts between their national, political and social institutions and the institutions of the other side.

C — Economic co-operation

20. In a desire to achieve economic co-operation on the widest scale, the two sides decided to broaden, intensify and strengthen co-operation in the following fields: (a) trade (b) mining and industry, (c) agriculture and animal husbandry, (d) energy and water resources, (e) transportation and telecommunications, (f) financial co-operation.

Trade

21. The two sides have decided to adopt the following necessary measures for this purpose: (a) to establish direct trade relations; (b) to meet the needs of their markets on priority bases as much as possible; (c) to facilitate direct African-Arab trade, including laying down detailed trade regulations; (d) to encourage and strengthen co-operation between the trade institutions, trade projects and participation in trade fairs; (e) to establish co-operation between the African and Arab banking institutions and the insurance and re-insurance institutions.

22. To achieve this, the two sides request the Administrative Secretary-General of the OAU and the Secretary-General of the Arab League to prepare studies on the African and Arab markets with the co-operation of the African Development Bank, the Arab Bank for Economic Development in Africa and the Economic Commission for Africa with a view to encouraging African-Arab trade.

Mining and industry

23. In accordance with the two sides' policy calling for the states' control on their natural resources and the achievement of the ideal value for their raw materials, the two sides have decided:

(a) to co-operate in the field of the regular surveying of natural resources for the purpose of developing their wise use;

(b) to intensify industrialization by way of exploiting, marketing and transporting their mineral and raw materials and to encourage investment projects in these fields;

(c) to develop financial and technical co-operation and to encourage research in all industry and mining fields and to reach an agreement on the appropriate conditions for this co-operation through the establishment of joint projects of the giving of grants and loans.

Agriculture, forests, fisheries and animal breeding

24. The two sides have decided:

(a) to develop agriculture by introducing modern and advanced methods in the fields of production, distribution and storage;

(b) to promote the modernisation of the methods of animal breeding, stock improvement and of animal raising;

(c) to guarantee the rapid and tangible increase in food production through direct investment, joint projects and the other means of production with regard to animal raising and food production, the utilization of forests and the marketing of timber products;

(d) to exchange information and the results of research to improve living conditions in the rural areas, while concentrating on the rural basic structures;

(e) to take the necessary steps within the framework of an acceptable system to help the African and Arab countries to process their raw materials to the maximum possible extent before their exportation;

(f) to reach an agreement on the preparations pertaining to financial and technical co-operation with the aim of attaining a joint action for developing agriculture, forests, fisheries and animal raising.

Energy and water resources

25. The two sides have decided to confirm the effective control by each state of the energy resources in its country.

26. The two sides have decided to reach an agreement among the states or the Arab and African specialized national establishments to:

(a) promote prospecting for all energy sources, including oil, and to exploit, transport and store them and to seek to develop investments in these operations;

(b) exchange information, expertise and technology in the energy field;

(c) promote the exchange of information and to use the

acquired expertise and the appropriate technology to improve climatic and desert conditions and also to promote the appropriate work methods pertaining to the utilization of rivers, lakes, basins and subterranean water sources;

(d) co-operate in exploiting hydroelectic energy and other sources of energy on a regional basis whenever possible for development purposes within the context of arrangements agreeable to the two sides;

(e) intensify the use of other energy resources such as solar, thermic nuclear and other sources of energy and also to intensify research in this field for the purpose of speeding up the process of economic development, halting desert sand drift and the erosion of sand, and combating drought in Africa.

27. In a desire to facilitate the means of communication between the African and Arab states, the two sides decided the following:

(a) to speed up the development of modern infrastructures for roads, railways, airways and inland waterways suitable for navigation as an important basis for the development of African-Arab co-operation;

(b) to establish connections, on priority bases, between the networks of roads, railways and national air routes with a view to facilitating the speedy, economic movement of people and goods in accordance with bilateral or multilateral agreements;

(c) to conduct the necessary studies for the establishment of unions for shipping companies to enable them to operate with greater efficiency, to participate in the use of port and maintenance facilities, and to explore the possibility of utilizing technical innovations in the fields of transportation and communications;

(d) to strengthen the ties of effective co-operation between airline companies with a view to extending the framework of air services and reorganizing them;

(e) to improve existing postal and telecommunications networks and to extend their framework on priority bases;

(f) to co-operate in implementing projects on regional and

continental levels in the fields of telecommunications, roads and railways.

Financial co-operation

28. The two sides decided the following:

(a) to adopt all the necessary measures to strengthen effective financial co-operation on terms that ensure security and guarantees through: (1) direct long-term bilateral loans with the best possible terms for both sides, direct investment and joint financial projects; (2) long-term multilateral loans with the best possible terms for both sides, financing of projects, including feasibility studies; (3) African and Arab participation in international financial consortia for the financing of joint projects in Africa and the Arab world;

(b) to facilitate the entry of African and Arab financial institutions in accordance with the applicable laws and regulations in force in the interested countries and on the bases of priority in the African financial capital markets;

(c) to call on the OAU and the Arab League to co-operate with the African Development Bank, the Arab Bank for Economic Development in Africa and other specialized institutions to find a suitable formula for closer economic, financial and technical co-operation, especially through the establishment of African-Arab financial institutions and the drawing up of an African-Arab agreement containing the bases for the treatment of investments;

(d) to call on the African Development Bank and the Arab Bank for Economic Development in Africa to co-ordinate their investment activity and participate in the financing of multi-faceted African projects.

D — Co-operation in the Social, cultural and educational fields

29. In a desire to achieve better understanding among the African and Arab peoples and states, the two sides agreed to strengthen ties in the social, cultural and educational fields by concluding suitable agreements on the following: (a) cultural

delegations and festivals; (b) education curricula and training and sports programmes; (c) workers and trade union activities; (d) co-operation in the field of information media, such as the press, news agencies, satellites used in communications, radio and television; (e) exchange of appropriate information and expertise and assistance in solving social problems such as the settling of nomads.

30. In view of the human and cultural role which tourism plays in promoting better understanding, the two sides also agreed to encourage and facilitate tourism and to strengthen co-operation, particularly through investments and joint projects, in this field.

E — Scientific and technical co-operation

31. The two sides decided the following: (a) to strengthen and co-ordinate research through the exchange of information and scientific and technical studies; (b) to establish joint consultative services and specialized training institutions; (c) to ensure direct technical co-operation which includes scholarships and grants for training in the fields of science and technology; (d) to extend the framework of technical co-operation to ensure the availability of experts.

THE INSTITUTIONS

32. In a desire to strengthen the co-ordination of African-Arab co-operation activities to contribute toward the implementation of this Declaration and Action Programme, the two sides decided:

(a) to establish a permanent joint committee on ministerial level to follow up and ensure the implementation of the provisions of this Declaration and to explore any other fields of co-operation periodically;

(b) each side to grant the other the status of observer in the meetings of every organisation discussing subjects of joint importance;

(c) the OAU and the Arab League each to establish as soon as possible representation at the secretariat of the other with a view to maintain closer and more permanent work relations in the implementation of African-Arab co-operation;

(d) to call on the African institutions and their Arab counterparts in the various spheres to adopt all the necessary measures to establish close working relations to facilitate co-operation and to co-ordinate their activity.

33. This Declaration was issued in Cairo on 9 March 1977. Its texts in the Arabic, English, and French languages are equally valid. And in testimony thereof we affixed our signatures.

INDEX